col03

D0018455

LIFE AND DEF

ALSO BY NELSON GEORGE

FICTION

Urban Romance

Seduced

One Woman Short

Show & Tell

NONFICTION

The Death of Rhythm & Blues

Elevating the Game: Black Men and Basketball

Buppies, B-Boys, Baps & Bohos: Notes on Post-Soul Black Culture

Blackface: Reflections on African-Americans and the Movies

Hip Hop America

Where Did Our Love Go?: The Rise and Fall of the Motown Sound

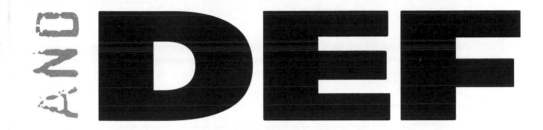

AND DEF

Russell Simmons
with Nelson George

THREE RIVERS PRESS
NEW YORK

Copyright © 2001 by Rush Communications, LLC

All rights reserved. No part of this book may be reproduced or transmitted in any form or by any means, electronic or mechanical, including photocopying, recording, or by any information storage and retrieval system, without permission in writing from the publisher.

Published by Three Rivers Press, New York, New York.
Member of the Crown Publishing Group, a division of Random House, Inc.
www.randomhouse.com

Three Rivers Press and the Tugboat design are registered trademarks of Random House, Inc.

Originally published in hardcover by Crown Publishers, a division of Random House, Inc., in 2001.

Printed in the United States of America

Library of Congress Cataloging-in-Publication Data
Simmons, Russell.
    Life and def: sex, drugs, money, and God / Russell
  Simmons with Nelson George.
      1. Simmons, Russell.   2. Sound recording executives and producers—Biography.
  3. Def Jam Recordings.   I. George, Nelson.   II. Title.
  ML429.S56 A3 2001
    338.4'7782421649—dc21
  2001028350

ISBN 0-609-80715-3

10 9 8 7 6 5 4 3 2 1

First Paperback Edition

921
SIMMONS
2001

This book is dedicated to my wife, Kimora Lee, and
my daughter, Ming Lee.
It is additionally dedicated to my father,
to the memory of my mother,
to my deeply artistic brothers Danny and Rev. Run,
and to the entire extended Simmons family.

RWS

CONTENTS

INTRODUCTION

When I was sixteen years old I almost killed somebody. His street name was Red, which he'd earned for his reddish yellow complexion and his nasty, devilish temper. Red had robbed me on 205th Street, which in 1973 was the drug supermarket of my Hollis, Queens, neighborhood. To support my taste for flashy clothes, I had been selling herb on 205th Street, just a few blocks from where my family lived.

Being robbed while selling drugs is an occupational hazard. And there was no embarrassment in being ripped off by Red— sticking up dealers on 205th Street was one of his criminal specialties. Still, there was a lingering question among my drug-dealing peers: If Russell sees Red, what's he gonna do? More than a question, it was a challenge—one I'd have no choice but to answer, one way or another.

Well, the answer came two weeks after Red robbed me. He came back on the block, apparently in search of his next victim. But before Red could make a move, we spotted him, and all the dealers started chasing him. We ran after Red for two or three blocks before a gang of us cornered him in the backyard of a single-family home. One of my niggas threw him down. A couple of the dealers sucker-punched him. And then, as Red struggled, somebody handed me a gun. "Let that nigga have it," someone said to me. It was the first (and only) time I've held a gun with the intention to shoot. I must have looked ready to bust a cap in him, because suddenly Red broke free of the three guys holding him and started climbing the backyard fence. Everything slowed down for me—now I was in the middle of one of those unexpected, scary, life-or-death moments. I held up the .45, aimed at Red's back and fired. My bullet sailed right over his head. The last I saw of Red were his feet swinging over the wall. I can still hear the voices of the dealers running through my head and feel the heat from the gun in my hand. It's a feeling I've never forgotten. I used to boast to all my drug-dealing homies that I'd just missed Red's ass and if I got another chance, I would've went up in him. But in my heart I knew missing Red was the best thing I ever did. The truth was that kid was just running toward a bullet anyway. Two weeks later Red and his brother were both killed in a botched liquor store robbery. I guess the owner was a better shot than me.

Sounds like a lyric from a rap by Slick Rick or Chuck D, right? Nah, it wasn't a song, it was my life. But it's the kind of real-life story that has inspired hip-hop's storytellers for over twenty years. That hip-hop embraces tales like mine—stories of decisions and danger with deep moral and emotional consequences—is one of the reasons it's grown so popular and I've had one of the greatest jobs in the world.

My life has largely been about promoting the anger, style, aggression and attitude of urban America to a worldwide audience. I have helped sell the culture of hip-hop by identifying, nurturing and promoting artists—rappers, comics, designers—who can take life-defining moments like my confrontation with Red and turn them into commercial products that, at their highest level, become objects of art. Instead of becoming a low-level criminal with a thick jacket of felonies and gunplay, I've taken the entrepreneurial energy I was putting into drugs and created a business that didn't even exist a generation ago. There were no rap stars when I was a teenager. There were no movies starring rappers or clothing lines bearing their names or, for that matter, books written by people involved with them. With the help of many I built the business of hip-hop from the ground up to a multibillion-dollar industry. There was no long-term vision then. We were all just making it up as we went along. But over time I developed a sense that this culture offered opportunities for economic, social and artistic growth like no other aspect of African American culture.

I don't expect everyone to agree with my views. In fact, I'm sure some readers will be hostile to the idea that hip-hop is a culture at all. I know aspects of the music, the fashion, the language and the politics of hip-hop offend many people. To those of you who feel that way, I just ask you to be open to hearing my story. To those of you who feel hip-hop in your souls, who love it as much as I do, kick back and chill with me. I'm just gonna tell you what I've seen, what I've experienced and what I've done, as honestly as possible. This is my story—a tale of life and def.

PART 1

HOLLIS TO HOLLY-WOOD

1 COLD GETTIN' PAID

There have always been two types of black businesses in this country. First, there are those like Johnson Publications or Essence Communications (or black hair care or cosmetics companies), which cater to black consumers and work that niche for all it's worth. *Ebony* and *Essence,* which are institutions in the black community, exist solely to target black consumers, draw revenue predominantly from the ad budgets of white corporations and portray a middle-class black version of American reality.

Then there's the Motown model. Berry Gordy labeled his company the "Sound of Young America." Gordy was a visionary who saw that black culture, as expressed through the music his company created, was just as viable and important culturally—and commercially—as anything in this country. Motown sold black pop music, written and performed by blacks, for consumption by all Americans regardless of their color.

My philosophy takes a little from both, yet differs fundamentally from them. Unlike *Ebony* or *Essence,* my audience is not limited by race. My core audience, my hip-hop audience, is black and white, Asian and Hispanic—anyone who totally identifies with and lives in the culture. Those are my peeps.

And unlike Motown, I don't believe in catering to the so-called mainstream by altering your look or slang or music. I see hip-hop culture as the new American mainstream. We don't change for you; you adapt to us. That's what has made Def Jam Records, *Def Comedy Jam* and Phat Farm, to name a few of my ventures, commercially successful and influential. And that is the central philosophy that has driven my career.

WHAT IS HIP-HOP?

I guess I should start with my definition of hip-hop. To me, hip-hop is modern mainstream young urban American culture. I know there's a lot of ideas there, but hip-hop's impact is as broad as that description suggests. Like rock and roll, blues and jazz, hip-hop is primarily a musical form. But unlike those forms of black American music, hip-hop is more expansive in the ways it manifests itself, and as a result, its impact is wider. The ideas of hip-hop are spread not just through music, but in fashion, movies, television, advertising, dancing, slang and attitude.

The beauty of hip-hop, and a key to its longevity, is that within the culture there is a lot of flexibility. So Run-D.M.C. and A Tribe Called Quest and N.W.A and Mary J. Blige and Luther Campbell and the Beastie Boys can all wear different clothes, use different slang and have a different kind of cultural significance. Yet all are recognizable as being part of hip-hop. I believe hip-hop is an attitude, one that can be nonverbal as well as eloquent. It communicates aspiration and frustration, community and aggression, creativity and street reality, style and substance. It is not rigid, nor is it easy to sum up in one sentence or even one book. Simply put, when you are in a hip-hop environment, you know it; it has a feel that is tangible and cannot be mistaken for anything else.

Hip-hop culture is, all these years later, closer to its original aesthetics than jazz or blues or rock and roll are to their roots. For example, the originators of rock and roll were black men who wore fly suits, had their hair slick and didn't give a fuck. That describes all those artists in the '50s who laid down the foundation, men who were trying to fight their way out of southern racism and northern poverty. In their time they were regarded as outlaws. They got arrested. They got harassed. They were attacked.

Eventually mainstream American took rock and roll and it changed. No longer rock and roll, it became rock. It became hallucinogenic. It became about rebellion for rebellion's sake. It was no longer about getting money and looking fly; it became about taking drugs and wearing dirty jeans. In the '60s and '70s, when this new rock emerged, the old music, and the old musicians, were tossed away. You couldn't tell this new audience that Chuck Berry and Led Zeppelin were the same thing. In one generation you were hot and then you were over.

Hip-hop, however, has been very consistent in its stance. A couple of years ago Erick Sermon, Redman and Keith Murray recorded the Sugarhill Gang's "Rapper's Delight," the first big rap hit from 1979, and did it exactly like the original. The concepts in that rap record from twenty-odd years ago are still valid. Hip-hop records are still about "I got a fly girl, I'm going to the motel in my new car." They still say, "I'm gonna get flak for being young and street. But I'm still gonna take a bite out of American culture. I'm gonna do it my way and I'm gonna buy everything in Bloomingdale's. I'm not into rebellion for the sake of rebelling. My rebellion has a goal—self-improvement, the ability to acquire all the things normally denied me or to change the way the world speaks, moves, dresses and thinks." So "Rapper's Delight," which basically borrowed rhymes from old-school pioneers, has the same aesthetic as you'd find on almost any Def Jam record today. Then it was gold chains. Now it's platinum Bentleys.

Which is why there are 40-year-old b-boys. I remember flying to a fight in Vegas and meeting the actor Ving Rhames and his wife. Turned out his brother was a competitor of mine in the old days who used to promote shows by DJ Hollywood and sell thousands of tickets. Ving and I talked about going to the Hotel Diplomat in Times Square, where we did big parties in the days before rap records. But we were also talking about the sound on a new Q-Tip record and how dope he was.

Ving and a lot of people like him are getting the same thing out of the culture they used to. The music isn't the same. Sometimes the language on the record is different. But it's the same take on American culture.

In the beginning we ran into a little bit of an obstacle when it came to communicating this urban black and Latino attitude to suburban America. Even after suburbanites began buying the music, they didn't really understand the aesthetic. Now, in the twenty-first century, it's come full circle. Suburbanites purchase hip-hop records in huge numbers, but they also have a deeper understanding of and appreciation for all aspects of the culture. As a result, hip-hop has influenced everything around them. Look at today's rock bands—Limp Bizkit, Kid Rock, Korn. They all have hip-hop running through their veins.

You know, rock stars used to be notorious for getting into brawls and getting drunk. In the '60s and '70s, when rock still had some guts, people like Mick Jagger and Jimmy Page represented youthful rebellion. They did drugs. They tore up hotel rooms. They made sexually suggestive records. They expressed sympathy for the devil. Now rap stars have taken it all to another level. They carry guns. They use guns. They go to jail. They express a connection to the people still in jail. They express solidarity with the people from their hood—no matter how dangerous it was or how much money they've made. They confront cops, politicians, other rappers and even themselves on record and off. They do all the things rock stars used to do and they do even more dangerous, outrageous things. Today a kid knows a rock star acts out because he's rebelling against his parents. A rap star, however, is doing it because he has a serious reason—discrimination, personal anger or ghetto conditions. And on top of all that, a rap star wants to make money and enjoy success, and is fearless in doing it. The result is the kind of attitude of authentic rebellion that rock was always supposed to have.

This stance has drawn criticism, but attacks on hip-hop have always been great for the culture. In fact, I personally want to thank Bob Dole, William Bennett and the rest of those right-wingers for reminding kids that hip-hop is theirs. When adults say, "Oh, fuck, don't listen to rap!" they just reinforce young people's commitment to it. Even some 40-year-olds who grew up on rap and who know that the messages in rap can be scary try to tell their kids, "Don't listen to it," which is like asking kids to buy it. People who grew up on rock now look at it and say, "Aw, it's okay," because it's not scary at all. Once that happens, kids don't want it and it becomes a museum piece.

On the other hand, black kids, and the core white, Asian and Latino kids into rap, don't listen to it just to piss off their parents. That kind of rebellion's irrelevant to them. They listen because it expresses what they're thinking about. Punk, new wave, alternative—most of it came and went. Today there's no Clash. There's no Nirvana. Right now rock can't fuck with rap—unless it adopts rap—because the culture is so raw and honest.

When rap came along in the late '70s, there was something synthetic about black pop music. The most popular black music of the time was R&B made simple for white people to dance to; they called it disco. Disco actually started within the gay dance community. They had a creative little thing happening, and then it crossed over to the mainstream. The record industry adopted it because it helped soften the edges of black music. But ultimately disco didn't address the issues rap has. Even though rap was born in the ghetto, it addresses issues a lot of kids across America (and the world) are dealing with—anger, alienation, hypocrisy, sex, drugs. All the basics.

Kids of all colors, all over the world, instinctively seek to change the world. They usually have this desire because they don't want to buy into the dominant values of the mainstream. Rappers want to change the world to suit their vision and to create a place for themselves in it. So kids can find a way into hip-hop by staying true to their instinct toward rebellion and change.

Hip-hop has, in fact, changed the world. It has taken something from the American ghetto and made it global. It has become the creative touchstone for edgy, progressive and aggressive youth culture around the world. That's why my business is bigger than it's ever been. And, I believe, we're far from through.

2 HOLLIS CREW

From my birth on October 4, 1957, to my early twenties, I spent most of my life in Queens, New York's biggest borough, the land of Archie Bunker, the Mets and eventually rappers, who put it on the map in a whole new way. Until I was eight my family lived in Jamaica, Queens, a large area in the center of the borough, whose main drag was Jamaica Avenue, a long, busy commercial thoroughfare with department stores, a huge old-style movie palace, a busy bus depot that linked city-run bus routes to the private bus lines that covered the far reaches of Queens, and the then-elevated J train line. One of my first memories is of walking down Jamaica Avenue under the J train tracks holding hands with my father, Daniel senior, and my mother, Evelyn. My father was a stocky, forceful man with a great, vibrant voice that could be both poetic and rough. My mother was a slender woman with sharp features and a sly, knowing smile. They'd met at Howard University in D.C., where he got a B.A. in history and she received degrees in sociology and psychology. So they were well educated and quite worldly. Neither of them was shy—each, in their own way, had a kind of charisma and a desire to express themselves. Even as a small child, I was aware of the creative energy they both radiated. There are no retiring people in the Simmons family—we are all creative, strong-willed, dynamic people.

My father was a schoolteacher and eventually attendance supervisor for District 29 in Queens. He was also very politically active—I remember walking in a picket line with him as a little boy over on Jamaica Avenue to protest discrimination in housing and employment. My father was very vocal about discrimination in New York and was involved with many civil rights organizations. His views about black empowerment and social activism played a big part in shaping how I view the world to this day. My mother spent much of her working life as a recreation director for the New York City Department of Parks. Growing up, I remember my mother being tough. I mean really tough. With three boys, she had to be. We weren't allowed to back-talk her or disrespect her in any way. Her scowl could hurt as deeply as a slap. At the same time she had a kind of sophistication about New York and the wider world that no one else in the family had. Her mother had been one of the first black nurses in New York and she'd been raised in Queens, so unlike a lot of black parents of that period, who'd come north from the South, my mother was a real big-city woman. She was also fine-featured and light-skinned, and had some of the haughty attitude that can go with that in the black community.

But my mother wasn't bourgie, because if she was, she'd never have married a true ghetto nigger like my father. My father is what you might call "culturally diverse." On one hand, he could recite from *Hamlet* and write insightful, sophisticated poetry. On the other hand, he could talk derisively all day about "pussy-lipped niggers"—boring, fake, plastic people who wanna distance themselves from the gritty core of African-American culture. My father was very well read and college educated, but that never made him feel he was superior to anyone. He really hated blacks he felt had an elitist attitude.

People don't know this, but my father wrote rhymes for several of Run-D.M.C.'s records, like "Thirty Days" and "You're Blind." To me, my father was a better poet than Run and a huge influence on him as a lyricist. My mother was a painter, so it's not surprising that my older brother, Danny, is also one. My mother's work was more structured and literal than Danny's, whose paintings have always tended more toward abstraction. My mother would draw your face so you recognized it, but with a curve or a twist in the approach that would personalize it as hers. If I had to compare her work to anyone's, I'd say it reminds me of Francisco Clemente, someone years later I've become good friends with.

But while both of my parents were artistic, they definitely didn't see eye to eye on art's role in a young man's life. My father thought art was good—but so was a college diploma and a nine-to-five job. My mother was much more of a free spirit—she felt that if you didn't want go to school and wanted to paint all day, that was all right too.

It's funny that I grew up surrounded by artistic people—my

parents, my brothers—since I've spent most of my life as an aide to and protector of artistic people. Certainly being in the center of all that creativity as a child deeply affected me. I believe what I've done in my life—in terms of helping artists develop and finding ways to market hip-hop culture—is itself profoundly creative work. My job has never been to simply throw a record out there hoping for a hit. It's working with artists to make sure the record reflects their view and also resonates within the community. Perhaps I've been good at working with artistic people because, from day one, those are the people I've always known.

ON 205TH STREET

In 1965 we moved to Hollis, a nice residential section of Queens that was 10 percent white. Right after we moved in that 10 percent disappeared. Hollis was filled with little two-story homes with driveways and small lawns. Hollis, along with Jamaica and St. Albans, were Queens neighborhoods where black people from all over the city moved once they got a little change in their pocket. We had people from the projects in Brooklyn, the tenements in Harlem and other parts of the city because you could own your own home with a loan from a credit union, giving you a feeling of suburban life while still within New York City.

My family's house was typical—two floors, an unfinished basement, an attic that my older brother, Danny, used as his bedroom. I split a bedroom with my little brother, Joey (later known as Run of Run-D.M.C.) on the second floor. We had a driveway and a garage, though the funny thing was the driveway was so narrow no cars could get through it into the garage. Growing up, we had two cars that I remember—a red Volkswagen and then, years later, a green secondhand Mercedes that everybody made a big deal over.

When we moved onto our block there was one white family left. They were directly across the street from us, and I guess my family was the last straw. They moved out soon after we moved in. It was a phenomenon typical of the '60s and '70s, when whites pursued a policy of self-segregation. The idea that blacks could afford to live next to them sent them running like roaches with the lights on.

It was on this block in Hollis that I met the people who would be my friends my whole life and learned the lessons, some good and quite a few bad, that would help shape me. As I entered adolescence in the early '70s, heroin culture was a dominant part of life in Hollis, just as it was in similar working-class neighborhoods all over the country. The influx of heroin that had started in the ghettos rippled out to working-class areas like Hollis, driven by aggressive drug dealers, police corruption and the desire for experimentation and danger that many young people feel. Drugs were a social force in that they affected how people viewed themselves and everyone around them. Drugs were an economic force that both drained working people of their money and empowered criminals. So despite my parents' being strong, hardworking role models and our living in a neat little home, my brother Danny and I got caught up in the dark side of ghetto culture.

Danny, who is four years older than me, was the Simmons family rebel. He felt the full impact of the '60s, with its championing of all kinds of social, sexual and political freedom. As a teenager, he wore American flag T-shirts (which were then seen as a sign of disrespect for Old Glory) and joined the Black Panthers. He got mad high. Danny took to calling the attic "the rocket ship" because he used to blast off up there, using acid as the fuel. There was a dresser by his bed, and every time Danny dropped acid he'd carve the date into the dresser with a knife. After a while that dresser looked like the wall in an Egyptian tomb. For a fledgling painter, acid was cool if you were just looking for some mind-expanding experimentation, but then Danny fell victim to heroin. Soon the rocket ship turned into needle park, because he'd bring friends up there to shoot up. Being close in age and very aware of drugs, I knew what was going on but kept quiet about it. Eventually, of course, it got out of hand and my parents made Danny leave the house. For much of his teen years Danny lived with my mother's mother in Jamaica. Since that period Danny has truly turned his life around. He runs two galleries—one in Manhattan, one in Brooklyn—runs our art charity and has a very successful career himself.

While Danny became a user, my indoctrination into drug culture came from dealing. Two blocks away from our house was 205th Street, which had the biggest drug trafficking scene in that part of Queens. It was a destination for dope fiends from all over, so dealers would be out there 24-7, moving heroin and weed like it was a McDonald's drive-through window.

But I didn't even have to walk those two blocks to understand the powerful lure of heroin. Down at the other end of my block lived Joe Morris, whose house often had a line of addicts waiting to cop that stretched from the front door all the way around the corner. At some point when I was a teenager I decided to get paid. People were making money all around me, so, like a lot of kids then and now, I began to sell weed. This decision wasn't made out of desperation or need. My family never missed a meal or came anywhere near being homeless. Part of it was peer pressure—many of my friends were doing it. Part of it was greed—as I'll talk about later in more detail, I always liked nice clothes and used this dope money to buy them. And finally, if you're selling, you never had to cop—you always had your own personal stash. So from my silly teenage perspective, selling on 205th Street made sense.

Once I'd made a connection and was really in the drug game, I'd sell on 205th Street and keep nickel bags of marijuana in the bushes in front of our house. I'd carry ten bags on me and keep twenty bags in the bushes in reserve. I'm sure my parents knew something was up. I believe my mother knew, and I know my father did once he found a thousand dollars in the house that he knew I didn't make on my job because I never had one.

For me selling was not about being glamorous or emulating *Superfly,* the big blaxploitation movie of that period. It was a way to get the things I wanted—things that in retrospect were ridiculous and unnecessary. My goal at that point, and for much of my teen years, was simple—to get into clubs where the fly kids hung out and to own fly clothes.

I loved A.J. Lester clothes. It was a clothing store that catered to urban taste for the flyest, latest, slickest gear: alligator and

lizard shoes, sharkskin slacks, Kangol caps, Blye knit sweaters, etc.
If it was upscale ghetto wear, it could be found at A.J. Lester's, the
official ghetto fly clothing store—and I, already quite caught up
in the glamour of street culture, wanted it all. I was as caught
up in having fly shit as any kid was then or now. My later interest in, and understanding of, street style and how to develop the
imagery of my acts all stem back to my fascination with being fly
as a teen.

I can't emphasize enough how reckless I was and how badly my
life could have ended up. I remember me and my friend Robert
Middleton, who also sold weed, smoking joints on Jamaica
Avenue in front of the library, our pockets bulging with nickel
bags, just two blocks from a police precinct house. Of course we
got arrested and ended up spending that night in jail. We were
both on probation for a year and a half after that.

Doing stupid shit like that was like auditioning for a big role
in the criminal justice system.

It takes a lot of hypocrisy to be a drug dealer. My favorite example is the pact I made with Roy Morris, the younger brother of
the block's dope dealer, Joe. Our pact was that we'd never "get
high." For us "getting high" meant shooting heroin, which older
guys like my brother Danny and Roy's brother Joe were doing. So
not getting high meant we could do any other kind of drug that
was available. It's that kind of half-assed thought process that
fucks people up to this day. Poor Roy ended up breaking his
promise and getting strung out. Eventually drugs led him to jail,
where he's spent most of the last twenty years. His brother Joe
ended up in jail for almost twenty-four years. Because of bad deci-

sions they made as teenagers, both of these men wasted the best part of their life behind bars.

Coming up, my parents made sure I went to P.S. 135, an integrated school that was in a white working-class area, instead of P.S. 134, the neighborhood school, which was attended overwhelmingly by blacks like my close friends from Hollis. For junior high I went to J.H. 109, another predominantly white school. So when we played softball against mostly black J.H. 92 we won, since the white boys knew how to catch and throw and play the game and the black kids didn't. But when we played basketball, J.H. 92 killed us. I'd be one of the only black guys on the J.H. 109 team, and I'd know everyone on the J.H. 92 team. The funny thing was that all the hustling, drug-selling niggas would bogart their way onto the school teams to play in the games and get uniforms, even when they barely went to class.

Getting me into integrated schools was one of the best things my parents ever did for me, but not because the schooling was automatically superior. Even at that age I was an observer of people. My friend Wendell says I've been a lifelong sociologist. Maybe it's in my DNA, since my mother studied the topic in college. All I can say for sure is that I saw immediately there are no differences between whites and blacks in terms of what they want out of life. Everybody wants to be liked. Most everybody wants to get high off something—herb, wine, beer, acid, heroin. Everybody wants to get laid. Sure, there are many cultural differences, but those differences usually cut across the obvious lines and have more to do with taste than race. I could play baseball with the white boys and basketball with the black guys, and I saw kinship

SIMMS LIBRARY ALBUQUERQUE ACADEMY

where others saw difference. Being able to see beyond the obvious when it comes to black and white would be key not just to my career but to my life.

The area I went to school in and Hollis were mirrors of each other. Same kinds of houses. Same kinds of cars. Same aspirations of the parents for their kids. Most of the white kids I went to school with ended up working for the post office or some other working-class gig, whereas my Hollis Crew friends ended up in jail or dead. Even as a teen, I used to wonder why there was so much visible damage from drugs in black neighborhoods and not in white areas of equivalent economic status. What was the difference? One thing I can point to is that heroin was sold openly in Hollis at places like Joe Morris's house and along 205th Street. But the police simply wouldn't allow that in white areas, while they let 205th, right near hardworking black families, become a supermarket where hard core black *and* white addicts came to cop. The easy access to heroin that law enforcement allowed truly contaminated our communities.

My brother Danny's generation was fucked up by drugs of every kind, since they experimented with anything they could get their hands on. There were definitely times my family worried Danny might not make it. Most of his friends didn't. Instead Danny matured into a successful painter and parent. Today he is president of the Rush Philanthropic Arts foundation, which donates hundreds of thousands of dollars to arts programs across the country. But Danny often reflects on all the gifted people he knew in the '60s who were ruined by addiction. My generation was damaged by heroin, angel dust and cocaine. I think the gen-

eration coming up now, coming up after crack, is better at resist-
ing drugs than any other generation I've seen. Most rappers on
Def Jam don't do hard drugs, and a few, like Jay-Z, don't even
smoke weed. They've seen what went on before and they'd rather
get paid than get high.

SEVEN IMMORTALS

Aside from my drug activities, I also was deeply involved with
another of young New York's early-'70s passions—gangs. At
around the same time I was selling drugs, I became a warlord in
the 17th Division of a gang called the Seven Immortals, which
gave me a position of leadership in a pretty loosely organized
group. This was an era when kids in gangs wore their dungaree
jackets inside out and drew an insignia on the back. We didn't
have guns and didn't kill people as gangs do today. The worst we'd
do was hit people with baseball bats and crack a skull or two.
Compared to current gangs with Uzis and Tec-9s, those were
more innocent times.

My friend Roy Morris and I were recruited by Willie Ward,
who was a few years older than us and could lead an angel straight
to hell with his charisma and confidence. He was from the Bronx
and brought the Seven Immortals to Queens. With Roy serving
as president of the 17th Division and me as warlord of that division, we helped build it up until we had at least two thousand
members. They ranged in age from 14 to 25, with most of the
members in the 14-to-16-year-old range. Our major activities

were breaking into school dances or concerts, either by throwing a brick through a window or by breaking through a door. We would ride on the subway and intimidate people if we could. But we were really young and not that fearsome.

I remember one day we rolled out to Coney Island intending to act tough and scare and rob people. Well, members of one of the roughest gangs in the city, the Black Spades, had been chillin' on the beach that day. When they heard we were around, they came looking for us. Now, most of the guys with us that day were 15 or 16 years old. The Black Spades were 30-year-old, jail-hardened gang vets. When they came looking, we scattered, taking off our jackets or wearing them so our gang insignia was inside. It was every man for himself, with all of us trying to get back to Queens. It was like the reverse of that movie *The Warriors,* where the Coney Island gang tries to get back home from the Bronx, except our destination was Hollis, Queens.

In retrospect I realize that my gang mentor, Willie, wasn't really respected by the hustlers his age in Hollis. Unlike the South Bronx or Bed-Stuy, Hollis really wasn't a big gang area. Hollis was a drug neighborhood, and the older guys in the Hollis Crew on 205th thought gangs were a sucker move. Willie himself, like many guys I knew, ended up coming in and out of jail about a million times.

My gang career ended not long after the murder of a Seven Immortals member named Big Bear. He'd been killed by the Seven Crowns, a gang out of Jamaica's toughest public housing, the 40 Projects. As a sign of contempt, they hung his colors up on a light flagpole in the park, which was one hell of a sight. But our reaction points out the difference between now and the '70s, because none of us was talking about which member of the Seven Crowns we were gonna kill in retribution. That drive-by mentality now so identified with street gangs didn't emerge until years later. At least I didn't have it. But the thing that hasn't changed about gangs is that for a lot of kids, especially the ones from broken homes, the Seven Immortals (like the Bloods and the Crips today) definitely filled a gap. Gang membership, then and now, provides a sense of family for a lot of people. I guess it hit me that I already had a strong family, so why was I risking my safety like this?

MY FLAVOR

I've never had dirty sneakers on in my life. Not when I was a teenager and not now. Back in the mid-'70s, when I was a teen, the sneakers to have were three stripe Pro-Keds we called 69ers. I had to travel far and wide to get them. Of course, the more inaccessible the garment, the better. In fact, at one point Keds stopped making them. You couldn't get them through regular distribution, which made me want them more. I had to find outlets that had surplus shoes, which meant traveling to Manhattan, the Bronx, Brooklyn or wherever I had to go to find them. Having them meant that much to me. They were a symbol of the pride I took in how I looked, which was crucial to my self-esteem—the same way certain sneakers, cars or high-tech toys are for young people now. I've always understood that desire (because I used to think the same way), so I've never judged young people as harshly as many adults do. It's one of the ways I've managed to bridge the generation gap between my consumers and myself.

I'd wear my 69ers with silk-and-wool pants that cost $32. I could have gotten similar pants with the same look for only $7. But the difference wasn't simply about money—it was about taking pride in your shit. At the time I thought having the right sneakers and pants meant I was a future Rolls-Royce nigga. Of course, what it really meant was that my values were warped, that my mentality was putting me at risk because of what I was doing to buy these things. To me the coolest stuff about American culture—be it language, dress or attitude—comes from the underclass. Always has and, I believe, always will. The problem is that street values are usually not nurturing. The street can teach you survival skills that are very useful. But they're not designed to help you grow as a spiritual being or mature as a whole person. It is that contrast between street knowledge and traditional values that frightens mainstream people about hip-hop and other forms of street expression.

The funny thing about me is that I've always been attracted to street shit—even though I could always see a lot of what was fucked up about it. There's an energy and creativity in the ways people from the street move, talk, think and react to situations I never get tired of. It's one of the reasons I have very little tolerance for plastic, stiff-ass, "pussy-lipped" (as my father calls them) black people.

For example, I loved spending summers in Baltimore with my cousins. They lived in a part of town that looked like a really, really worn-down part of suburbia with poorly kept houses and yards.

When people think of Baltimore they think of the row houses. When I think of Baltimore I think of where my cousins lived. I also think of rats. There were so many of them near my cousins' house, we spent our nights throwing rocks at them for fun. Chasing after rodents with intent to kill may not strike you as the most wholesome activity for young people, but I had a great time because it was fun—and risky, since rats do bite and they sure carry diseases.

To me the worst summer vacation I ever had was when I was a teenager and my father sent me to a camp upstate. The place was full of nice, middle-class, well-behaved Negroes who had no alcohol and weed stashed away. I'm sure they were all lovely people. But in my opinion they weren't creative or fun or at all exciting. I didn't last two weeks in Camp Bore-Me-to-Death before I came back to Hollis.

As a teen, my musical taste was forming, and it reflected my overall attitude toward life. I liked gutsy, cool music, nothing too pop. A lot of that had to do with radio reception. I could get the black AM station WWRL very well, since it broadcast out of Woodside, which is a section of Queens. 'RL was a hard-core R&B station with jive-talking DJs who damn near rapped the ads for hair-straightening potions and no-money-down credit. 'RL played classic soul vocal groups like the Dells, the Dramatics, the Moments, the Detroit Emeralds, Blue Magic and Black Ivory. This wasn't like the pop stuff you'd hear on WABC, the big AM Top 40 station in town that played Motown, sweet R&B and white pop. I mean, the Supremes were okay. I didn't like the Four Tops. I could get with the Temptations a little bit because David Ruffin was cool as a motherfucker.

The music I liked was very ghetto and gritty. It was the stuff that didn't really cross over much, but spoke to a roots black experience. People don't understand this now, but the falsetto, crying singers were the most ghetto back then. For all their talk of love, there was something very pimplike, manipulative and fly about that sound. Like one of my favorite records, "Hey Love," by the Delfonics, where the lead singer was begging for that ass in roof-scratching falsetto—that's what I related to, that's what moved me. In the late '80s with Oran "Juice" Jones, Chuck Stanley and Alyson Williams I made records in that same tradition on Def Jam. They didn't all sell, but they were true to my taste in music and the aesthetic that has always attracted me.

COCA LEAF INCENSE

For my father, everything I was into—drugs, gangs, slick clothes—meant I was heading straight to prison. So my senior year in high school my father, irritated by my bullshit, got me a job at the Orange Julius on Sixth Avenue and 8th Street in Greenwich Village, which is now the location of a papaya juice store. To this day that job, at a fast-food juice spot that still serves thirsty teenagers in the heart of the Village, has been the only nine-to-five of my life.

Getting away from Hollis was good. It allowed me to see a wider world. The Village, with its mix of blacks and whites, gays and straights, real bohemians and experimenting weekend bridge-and-tunnel tourists, would influence very much my vision of selling hip-hop later. It, along with SoHo, would be one of the places I would live in the future where I'd see not the differences in people, but the kinship among everyone. The attitudes that connected them is where the opportunity to sell to them existed. I didn't know that yet. But what I did see then was all kinds of people walking past that store, wearing all kinds of clothes and manifesting an incredible range of attitudes. I was always an observer, and my time at Orange Julius gave me a chance to see stuff that just wasn't happening in Hollis.

At the time, of course, I didn't realize the value of all that. Instead I found myself seduced by the wonders of coca leaf incense. At a store on 8th Street next to the Orange Julius, coca leaf incense was sold from under the counter, even though it was a perfectly legal product. But, as one of my drug dealer friends showed me, if you chopped it up and placed it in aluminum foil, it acted and looked like cocaine. Even better for the deception was that if you put this stuff in your mouth, your whole face froze up. The caffeine in it gave you a bit of a rush, too. If you didn't know better—and how many people on the street could afford real coke?—you'd think you had real cocaine. Though I never would steal or rob people—particularly after that shooting incident in Queens—I had no problem selling fake cocaine to whoever came along in Harlem or Greenwich Village. In fact, I lived high on the hog selling that stuff for two years.

Of course, the beauty of coca leaf incense was that if you got arrested, so what? I remember getting arrested on 4th Street with a huge box of the stuff. The cops knew I was selling it—what else would you do with a large quantity of incense?—but they had to let me go because there's no law against selling coca leaf incense. It was something anyone could purchase at stores in downtown New York.

The real danger was not the law—it was someone figuring out they'd paid cocaine prices for beat shit. People got shot over simple misunderstandings like that. I was lucky that never happened to me. I mean, I got robbed three or four times while selling it—an occupational hazard—but never caught a beat-down from someone complaining about the product.

When I first started selling fake cocaine, someone told me one of my customers had died. That freaked me out. Then I ran into the guy who was supposed to be dead. I asked him how the coke was, and he said, "I loved that shit you sold me. I cooked it, and soon as it turned green, I shot it up." It's funny—I was so relieved he wasn't dead, but not fazed at all that the guy was mainlining coca leaf incense.

It must have been frustrating to my parents to see me wasting my time out in the street. But I didn't think selling coca leaf incense was drawing me deep into a criminal mentality. I thought I was very clear about my limits. But looking back, I can see how lucky I was. I never sold heroin. I was never arrested holding anything heavy, and none of the four or five times I got robbed dealing did I get shot or stabbed.

The sad thing is how many of my Hollis Crew peers were killed by the drug lifestyle. Some got hit in the head by thieves one time too many. Some got shot. Some died of AIDS in jail. The common denominator was drugs—they were killed pursuing a high or selling a high, by an addict or by their own addiction.

In contrast, I remember this kid Roby. He was well known in our hood because his mother had a signal for when she wanted him to come home. She'd flash the lights in their house twice and it was time for him to come in. Of course, all us cool 205th Street niggas used to laugh at him. The guy was kind of a joke on the block. Just saw a picture of him in a paper the other day, and it wasn't an obituary. Roby was named a chief in the fire department. Most of the guys who made fun of him are dead. Draw your own conclusions.

3 THE FORCE

The New York City that created hip-hop wasn't the one we live in today. The Big Apple back in the mid-'70s wasn't the strictly policed, prosperous, yuppified place it is today. Middle-class people were leaving in droves. Johnny Carson was on every night cracking Central Park mugging jokes. There were transit strikes, teacher's strikes and a crazy night all the lights went out. Landlords were torching the South Bronx, and Harlem was best known as the home turf of the city's "Mr. Untouchable," dope kingpin Nicky Barnes.

Even the school I started attending in 1975, City College of New York, in Harlem, was viewed as a symbol of what was wrong with New York. City College had open enrollment, which guaranteed every student in the city a shot at college. This flooded the school with black, Latino and immigrant kids, something resented by the old alumni. Within all this negativity, the most influential pop culture of the last part of the twentieth century was born. I must admit my entry into this culture didn't come in the most wholesome manner.

It started in the last semester of my senior year in high school, when my friend Robert Middleton and I would take LSD every Friday. Usually we'd do it after school; we'd drop acid, and suddenly Mickey Mouse would be chasing us down Jamaica Avenue. Compared to taking heroin and nodding out, acid was like taking a trip, like going to the Village from Hollis. We'd take that stuff and trip all weekend.

One morning Robert and I were just coming down from an acid trip when my man Bud, a tall, lean guy who was a charter member of the Hollis Crew, came over with this new drug that was hot uptown. It was called angel dust, and the bag was stamped Red Devil. Though I didn't know it yet, angel dust would become my drug of choice. In the fall of 1975, when I entered City College, Harlem, like most ghettos then, was full of dust, so school gave me many chances to increase my appreciation.

For you students of urban history, angel dust, or PCP, was the big recreational drug of the late '70s and early '80s. It wasn't a cool rush like cocaine or trippy like acid, but it did something to your head that was unique to each person. Personally, I loved getting "dusty." It made me happy. For real, however, it could have dangerously unpredictable consequences. Angel dust was so powerful that people would smoke it and get crazy enough to jump off a building or take on twelve cops and not feel the blows.

Dust was everywhere uptown, and there were many competing brands. When dust made you violent, the police didn't just arrest you. They'd take you to Harlem Hospital and shoot you up with

Thorazine. All the Thorazine was supposed to do was calm you down. But the combination of PCP and Thorazine would fry your brain and have a lingering effect. People who got shot with the Thorazine treatment would talk slow and have a seemingly permanent lethargic look about them. The police used to have teams out there looking for dust heads like we were zombies in some bugged-out urban horror flick. When you were high off Red Devil, you did your best to avoid the cops and Harlem Hospital. While attending City College, I maintained my angel dust ritual, but instead of going home to Queens, I'd hang out in the student lounge at City College until eleven or twelve at night and then roll over to Charles' Gallery on 125th Street, a club in the late '70s that was one of the first to cater to young people and the emerging new music scene.

It was in the CCNY student lounge that I met Rudy Toppin, aka Rudy Spli, one of the most influential people in my life. It was Rudy who nicknamed me Rush and got me into promoting shows, so he played a big part in shaping my identity. Rudy was attending City College and received BEOG, a form of financial aid where you got a check for $600 or so every semester. Back then $600 for a college student was a lot of cash. People would get the check, think they were rich and stop going to classes. Aside from collecting his BEOG checks, Rudy's main interest was working as a promoter at Charles' Gallery. Calling him a promoter may be overstating his original involvement, since basically all Rudy did was give out flyers. Still, it allowed him to get into the club for free, which made his gig attractive to me.

Rudy was a slick Harlem nigga who'd hang in the student

lounge and then spend hours snapping on anybody who walked by. Rudy and his crew were slick in a different way than the Hollis Crew. They weren't into the Blye knits and A.J. Lester slacks that took up most of my money, but they had an organic Harlem cool that a Queens guy like me aspired to. No matter how much fly gear I bought or how much cool I tried to project, I was from Queens and Rudy was from Harlem, the spiritual home of urban culture. I could aspire to having the aura of a Harlemite, but for Rudy it came natural and smooth.

Hanging out with Rudy at Charles' Gallery is what led me to my first hip-hop experience. As I said, Charles' Gallery catered to a young crowd by using young DJs, unlike a lot of spots uptown that either had jazz or R&B bands or aspired to be low-rent Studio 54s. On this particular night it was Easy G on the ones and twos, cutting up the kinds of records kids were into uptown. But the real revelation was the "world-famous" Eddie Cheeba rhyming to get the crowd excited. I don't know about the crowd, but shit, it got me excited.

Most of what he performed were simple rhymes to get people to dance and make noise ("Somebody, anybody, everybody scream!") plus lines about how fly he was. Most of the crowd had heard Cheeba before, so they chanted along or responded with their bodies, moving harder to the beat because the MC said so. It wasn't a sophisticated rhyme flow by current standards. But hearing Cheeba in '77 made me feel I'd just witnessed the invention of the wheel.

Just as shooting at Red and missing let me know, happily, that I had no future in real crime, watching and hearing Cheeba had an equally powerful effect. I was standing there in a room full of peers—black and Hispanic college kids, partying and drinking—and it hit me: I wanted to be in this business. Just like that I saw how I could turn my life in another, better way. All the street entrepreneurship I'd learned selling herb, hawking fake cocaine and staying out of jail, I decided to put into promoting music. It seemed a lot less dangerous, more fun and more prestigious. Just like that, I decided I no longer would be involved in something like drug dealing that risked my life.

With Rudy as my partner, I started investing my hard-earned money into renting venues and negotiating with acts. I was still taking drugs—that wouldn't be curtailed until years later—but I was no longer selling them, which surely helped the quality of my life. It was amazing to realize how much the long hours on the streets and the harassment by police and stickup kids had affected my demeanor. Once out of that game, I felt better about myself and related to the world differently. I was more relaxed, happier and not as edgy. No matter how intense a negotiation was with an MC or his manager, it never felt as dangerous as standing in an alley trying to convince a stranger to buy fake cocaine.

Starting to promote was great for my spirit, though it had a terrible, ultimately fatal effect on my schoolwork. I actually did more schoolwork while selling drugs. Maybe I started fucking up in school because I felt I'd already found my life's work. What was the point of chemistry when I knew my job was to sell tickets?

Eventually I left City College in my senior year, just four or five credits short of a sociology degree. This really upset my father, who thought I was a fool. Over and over he lectured me that the only way for a black man to make it was to get a degree and a job. For a while there I felt like I was a failure in my father's eyes, which hurt a lot, but promoting felt right in my gut. I knew that to be a man I had to follow my heart. My mother was always more open to Danny, Joey and me pursuing a more nontraditional, entrepreneurial way.

Early in my promoting career I lost all the money I'd saved putting on a show in Harlem no one came to. I came out to Hollis and no one would help me. My father just wanted me to go back to school and told me so. What could I say? I had no money. Then my mother went back in the house and came out with $2,000 in crisp $100 bills from her personal savings. It was that money that kept me afloat until Kurtis Blow broke and I entered the record business. That act of love and faith, which is what kept me in business at a key time, is my favorite memory of her.

HOLLYWOOD

In the world of promoting rap shows for black teenagers in the late '70s there was a real hierarchy. There was Eddie Cheeba, Luvbug Starski and others at that level. But they were all beneath DJ Hollywood. A lot of people say a lot of things about who started what in hip-hop and who played at this park or that. But the bottom line is that to me Hollywood was the biggest figure in that era of hip-hop, because he was the man people would pay to see.

Hollywood could play Club 371 in the Bronx. He could play at the Diplomat Hotel in Times Square. He could play at a party at Jones Beach before five thousand people. In the days before hip-hop records were being made, Hollywood expanded the market in New York for MCing and break beats. Anywhere in the five boroughs Hollywood played, he could entertain and move the crowd. Hollywood's name always went at the top of the flyer whenever a show was being promoted. Just because he played inside clubs and giant halls for paying customers didn't make what he did any less creative, rebellious, hip or hot than the DJs and MCs who played in the park. It just made him bigger.

Hollywood was a chunky, jolly guy who'd been in vocal groups until he went solo as an MC. His voice was deep, rich and joyous. And he communicated that inner vibrancy like no one before or since. Whatever was fun, fresh and dynamic about this new scene, Hollywood epitomized it. Like most MCs of the day, Hollywood could DJ as well as rap. But he was at his very best with a DJ like Starski working with him, freeing him to do nothing but talk. Of all the party rockers, Hollywood was the best entertainer, but all the DJs and MCs knew that what they were doing uptown in the Bronx and Harlem was radically different from what was going on in suit-and-tie black downtown clubs like Leviticus.

It's so appropriate that Chic's "Good Times" was used by the Sugarhill Gang on "Rapper's Delight," the first recorded rap hit. Chic had become well known by doing disco records, but "Good Times" reflected the new aesthetic even if Chic's Nile Rodgers and Bernard Edwards didn't know it when they made the track. It had simple melody, a memorable hook and an incredible bass, guitar and drum arrangement that b-boys could instantly relate to. Not only was it a great single, but it spawned many other records (Vaughn Mason's "Bounce, Rock, Skate, Roll," Kurtis

Blow's "Christmas Rappin'," Queen's "Another One Bites the Dust," Kool & the Gang's "Ladies' Night") that were used by DJs and MCs to spread the aesthetic.

Whether you were in a park in the Bronx or a club on Lenox Avenue, there was a certain sensibility Hollywood and all the other young MCs and DJs shared. If you were playing for this teenage, uptown crowd, you didn't put on dance records by the Village People or Cerrone. You'd play the first eight bars of Bob James's "Take Me to the Mardi Gras" or James Brown's "Funky President" or do a mix of Eddie Kendricks's "Girl, You Need a Change of Mind" or the Incredible Bongo Band's "Apache." These parties were built around records that either weren't on the radio in New York, were from a different era or style (jazz, rock, or funky '60s James Brown) or were being mixed and cut up in ways Frankie Crocker, the city's number one radio DJ on the urban contemporary station WBLS, and the other radio people simply couldn't understand.

KNOWLEDGE ME

Just like Hollywood has not been given his due in the history of hip-hop, I feel another smaller but important influence has been overlooked—the Five Percent Nation of Gods and Earths. The Five Percenters are members of a religion that developed in jail among black inmates from the New York area. In fact, let me put it this way—if the Nation of Islam is a religion that finds converts in prison, Five Percenters find their converts *under* the prison. That's how street it is. It began as an offshoot of the Nation of

Islam, but it never had the discipline or strong organizational structure of the NOI. Based around the idea that the black man was God and that only 5 percent of us had true knowledge of self, it's been very influential over the years in the young black community because it was very much a religion about talking.

Slick, smooth-talking, crafty niggas gravitated to it because the Five Percent religion's membership was built on the ability of its members to articulate their devotion to a strict set of beliefs with as much flair as possible. A true Five Percenter could sit on a stoop or stand on a street corner and explain the tenets of the sect for hours on end—and be totally entertaining! The Five Percent religion elevates black men, telling them they're all gods here on earth but only 5 percent are true believers. A Five Percenter will says some fly shit like "I've got seven moons, three suns and two earths." It sounds mystical, but he's really talking about all his women, with his two earths being his closest girls. Not only was their rap hot, but phrases like "knowledge me," "true mathematics," "two degrees of knowledge," and "droppin' science" are just some of the linguistic contributions the Five Percent religion made to hip-hop. Street names like True God, U-God, Wise Allah and Divine Intelligence emerged because of how Five Percenters labeled themselves.

Listen to rappers from Brooklyn or the Queensbridge projects, like Nas, and you hear Five Percent–speak all in their rhymes. Rakim's poetry is immersed in it. A lot of the poetic images in hip-hop are informed by them, from "Eric B. Is President" (in his three references to seven MCs, which relates to Five Percenter beliefs) up to Erykah Badu's "On and On." The Nation of Islam is more visible and respectable in terms of its presentation, and is clearly more powerful than the Five Percenters as an organization. However, during the period when the gangs I hung with in the '70s gave way to '80s hip-hop culture, it was the street language, style and consciousness of the Five Percent Nation that served as a bridge.

THE TRACK

As I started to grow my business, I watched how other promoters were handling their operations. Jerry Roebuck is now best known for promoting the huge Black Expos that have been institutions in the African-American community for almost two decades, but back in the day Jerry was a party promoter. He would give out flyers to his events with headlines that read, "Jerry Roebuck in association with Harold Maynard [another promoter] and Reggie Wells [a top DJ]." So I started headlining my flyers "Rush Productions in Association with Rudy Toppin and Kurtis Blow." I became Rush, "the force in college parties," which gave my shows an identity. Guess it was an early example of branding.

Kurtis Blow, aka Curtis Walker, who went to City College with me, was the first artist I managed and would also be the first rapper signed to a major label. He was a smooth, handsome Harlem native with a booming low tenor voice and real charisma. He was first known as Kool DJ Kurt, but I gave him the name "Blow" because long after everyone else had stopped, Kurtis was still selling coca leaf incense as cocaine. By then stores no longer had it under the counter. Now it was on top of the counter. Everybody and their mother knew about the scam. But Kurtis still sold it, right up until he made records. Calling him "Blow" was also a bite on Eddie Cheeba's handle, something Eddie never liked, and it's one reason he was never enthusiastic about doing shows I promoted.

By 1977 our club promotions started blossoming, and we were working in a lot of venues. One of the hottest was Small's Paradise, the old Harlem jazz club off 135th Street that Wilt Chamberlain once owned, where we promoted a night called Terrible Tuesdays. Competition uptown grew fierce around '77 because rapping DJs got really popular and started to challenge traditional DJs and bands for gigs. This was the disco era, so people were already used to going to clubs not to see a band, but to see a DJ. Now hip-hop added a charismatic MC, someone who kept the party going. That added more value for your dollar. Club owners started to notice that an MC and a DJ drew bigger crowds than just a local band or a DJ, especially when they were trying to attract a younger black crowd.

A "track" developed of places you could work in Manhattan—City College, Small's Paradise, Hunter College, Charles' Gallery, the Renaissance Ballroom, Club 371 and Broadway International. And the audiences on this track didn't get bored, because even though there was an MC on the mike, you were under no obligation to stand and watch him. It was still a party. You could dance, drink, get busy or all of the above.

This was a whole different world from the downtown disco world of progressive clubs like the Paradise Garage and the Loft or midtown black bourgie clubs like Leviticus or Justine's. Those were the venues the uptown b-boys were—in their choice of clothes, music and attitude—rebelling against. In New York at this time, uptown and downtown were two different worlds. The black club scene downtown was about aping white disco and crossing over to white taste. Our scene uptown was about being our ghetto selves. I was learning important lessons—that being on the edge was where the excitement and creativity were, and that to be successful, you had to be true to your audience. Simple, but not obvious if you weren't paying attention.

The only people who knew or cared about the hip-hop track were the b-boys. There was no press coverage. No TV. No radio. No one outside of this community paid any attention to what was going on until after "Rapper's Delight" came out. So word of mouth was important, but you still needed to promote to make a real impression. The more flyers you were on, the more stickers and posters you could have stuck on walls or street lamps, the more popular you became as a promoter. Because the competition in Manhattan was so thick, Rush Productions began doing shows in Queens. We billed Kurtis as "Queens' #1 rapper," though he was a Harlem native and at the time didn't know Jamaica from Flushing. Early on we learned the value of hype and creating mystique. A Harlem MC working in Queens in '77 was the equivalent of a New York MC in LA in '83. It was a must-see for any hip-hop fan.

At that time Kurtis was a soloist, spinning and rapping at the same time. Obviously it was difficult to mix, keep the beat and rap at the same time, so he favored records that had longer instrumental sections or breaks. MFSB's "Love Is the Message" has a great three-minute break that Kurtis would just rap over. One reason that record became a hip-hop classic was because every young

DJ who wanted to rhyme but didn't have great mixing skills would drop that on and only have to change it twice in six minutes.

Hollywood, Cheeba, Starski and Reggie Wells were all MCs who were way ahead of Kurtis in terms of celebrity. Kurtis really didn't get ghetto famous until he hooked up with Grandmaster Flash in late '77. When I started booking Grandmaster Flash, he would bring some, but not all, of his Furious Five MCs to Queens from the Bronx, where he was already a legend. Eventually Kurtis Blow became Flash's unofficial sixth MC. That was very important to Kurt, who gained some credibility in the Bronx through this association. In my eyes the great Grandmaster was the DJ from the park youth scene who was most ready to grow to adult ballroom status. Kool Herc, Bambaataa, Grand Wizard Theodore and many others were great creative stars, but they played in a different world from the one I aspired to promote in. They were the b-boys who played the high school gyms, where there was more angel dust (which I liked), more fighting and less money (which I didn't). I'm the first to admit that I am not an authority on their influence, but these stars were more DJs than MCs. They were also younger and less profitable than a Hollywood or Cheeba was.

Flash's main indoor venue up until then was a Bronx place called the Sparkle, where Big Bank Hank, later to be part of the Sugarhill Gang, was a bouncer. So we said, "Get down with us. You bring your Bronx fans. Kurtis brings his Queens fans. We then promote with all that clientele in our pocket." We did two shows back to back—one in Queens, one in Manhattan—and got out fifteen thousand flyers in the streets and a couple of thousand stickers in the subways. I remember Kurtis walking from 155th

Street to 110th Street on Broadway just giving out flyers. I did a similar stroll through Queens. Way before street teams started putting up snipes (aka posters) on walls around the city, the people who worked for Rush Productions were walking the streets to sell our promotions.

The first show was Flash's first appearance in Queens. It was at the Fantasia, a tough spot near a housing development known as the 40 Projects in Jamaica. The 40 Projects would produce some of the city's legendary black gangsters—like Fat Cat Nicholas and "Pappy" Mason. These guys were the drug kingpins for our generation. While Nicky Barnes was a king in Harlem—he got so big Jimmy Carter ordered him taken down after reading about him in the *New York Times*—these guys were new gangsters, steeped in the new street culture. They had Kangols and big jewelry and looked as hip-hop as Kurtis or Flash. So the crowd that night was rough, but they loved hip-hop and formed a mob outside the Fantasia. Flash was that much of a legend in the streets. And remember, this was four years before he made a record.

We'd work a lot in the Fantasia after that. The Kurtis Blow–Flash combination really was hot in Queens. Then in '78 we had a problem. We'd done well at the box office and were leaving the Fantasia late one night. When we stepped into the street, bullets started flying—stickup kids were trying to rip us off for the gate. I remember ducking under a car and holding on to the money as guys ran by looking for us. That was my last show at the Fantasia.

The next night we were at the Hotel Diplomat in Times Square, and that was wild, too! The Diplomat was a run-down spot on 43rd Street between Sixth and Seventh that was clearly on its last legs, since they were letting a bunch of black teenagers do shows there. Down the block on the same side of the street was Xenon, which was the number two glam disco of the time, right behind Studio 54. Xenon was the place you went to do coke if you couldn't crash 54. It had a velvet rope, limos lined up, a picky doorman, the whole nine. Across the street was Town Hall, a nice sedate concert venue where folk singers and jazz musicians performed.

Suddenly 43rd Street was jammed with b-boys, pouring in from Times Square on the Seventh Avenue end and off the D train from uptown at Sixth Avenue. The result was a mini-riot. You had people getting robbed, mugged, stomped, trampled. Outside the Diplomat you had a clash between all these different groups of party people on the street and people desperately trying to get into the Diplomat. It was a mess outside, but as always, the show still went on. At the Diplomat they had bulletproof box offices, so Kurtis and I escaped there that night. Not surprisingly, we had a lot of trouble getting security companies to work with us. We'd get a company for one promotion, and that was it. The next company would do one show and then they'd quit, too.

Eventually Kurtis hired my little brother, Joey, who we called "DJ Run his disco son," to work the turntables for him. At that point Run was 13 years old. After a year and a half working with Kurtis, Run broke his arm, and Kurtis found a new DJ, Davey D, a kid from Queens with twelve crates of records, which was a serious accomplishment at the time. Flash had seventeen crates and Afrika Bambaataa had twenty, so twelve made Davey D a contender. Davey wasn't just a DJ, but a real musician who played guitar and other instruments. Not only did he become Kurtis Blow's first DJ, but he'd later play on and produce a lot of influential records, including his solo hit "One for the Treble." But the time we spent working with Flash was crucial to building Kurtis's, and Rush Productions', credibility in the growing scene.

4 MAKING RECORDS

My first contacts with the world of the adult music business weren't too fruitful. All the black people in the business in the late '70s were true R&B people. They thought R&B was all commercial black music was or could ever be. Plus they were all in their late twenties and older, and treated us young hip-hop promoters as kids who were just playing at being in the business. Even before hip-hop was really a force on vinyl, you could see a real generation gap between the black adult world and the young black culture that spawned hip-hop.

My first experience with this attitude came with a guy who went by the name of Saint Saint James (he named his son Saint Saint Saint James), who was the booker at Club Hollywood and a consultant for Club 371. Saint was one of the many black gatekeepers hip-hop had to go through to grow. And unfortunately, like a lot of those people, he just saw us as kids off the street. We wouldn't be around for long, they thought, so why treat us with respect?

Once I gave Saint $1,900 for a show I wanted to promote at Club Hollywood with Evelyn "Champagne" King and Hollywood, and he straight up stole it. Just took my $1,900 and disappeared.

The irony of that story is that years later Saint James ended up working for me at Rush Management and Def Jam, doing independent promotion and getting my records played on stations along the East Coast. I had no bitterness toward him. I needed Saint's contacts, and by then he needed a check. Holding a grudge against him would have been easy. But the fact that Saint knew me early on actually made him work aggressively for me later. There may have been some guilt involved, but there was also a certain pride there, too. He knew how far I'd come and now respected me for hanging in there. I never trusted him completely, but I felt now he was gonna use his tricks for me. I try very hard not to hold grudges—the guy you hate today could easily be working for you tomorrow. If you stick around long enough in this business, everything comes full circle.

My first positive encounter with the recording industry turned out to be my most important. Robert "Rocky" Ford worked in *Billboard* magazine's production department, but he was very visible in the R&B music scene because he also contributed articles and reviews on black music to *Billboard*, the industry's number one trade publication. Rocky lived with his mother in St. Albans, the Queens neighborhood right next to Hollis, which is why Rocky was walking down Jamaica Avenue one afternoon in 1978 and saw my brother Joey hanging up posters for one of my parties in Queens. Rocky asked Joey about Rush Productions and gave him his card. I called Rocky and we hooked up. Turned out he was doing a story on what were called "b-beats," or break beats, and rapping DJs. Through his contacts in retail, Rocky had noticed other flyers and heard about DJs looking for beats in obscure records. Rocky's story in *Billboard* would be the first national coverage of hip-hop.

But Rocky wasn't just a writer. He'd worked in advertising before he got with *Billboard* and had a good eye for a strong idea. Behind his glasses and his unruly curly Afro, there was a keen mind. Way before most adults, Rocky saw potential in this emerging scene. So after hanging out at some of our promotions and seeing how the scene was developing, Rocky got the idea to make a rap record. The only problem was that he was stuck on recording Eddie Cheeba. Rocky was always talking Eddie Cheeba this, Eddie Cheeba that. Of course, he'd heard of Cheeba more often than he had of Kurtis. That all changed when he saw Kurtis at the Diplomat on August 31, 1979. Kurtis was on fire that night. His rhymes were flowing. His Afro was tight. He just looked and sounded like a star. It didn't hurt that he was performing with Grandmaster Flash. After seeing Kurtis that night, Rocky decided he wanted to use him instead of Cheeba for his record.

Rocky also influenced Kurtis to let me manage his recording career. Kurtis was my man, but I was just a party promoter with no experience outside that field. Not surprisingly, Kurtis felt that Rocky, because of his age and *Billboard* background, should have been handling him in this new area. But that really wasn't Rocky's thing.

Yes, he would aid in guiding Kurtis, and he often used his contacts to help us, but he convinced Kurtis that my energy and commitment were what he needed on a day-to-day basis. Rocky's confidence in me at that moment really helped me grow and expand my reach. A few years later Rocky would, like Saint James, come work for me at Rush Management. Both men were mentors—one introduced me to the dark side, the other to the light—and both proved useful to me later. I believe all experiences, good and bad, have the capacity to mold you and make you stronger. You learn from all of it.

Rocky and J. B. Moore, an advertising salesman at *Billboard* who wanted to produce, got the idea for Kurtis to cut a single called "Christmas Rappin'," figuring the novelty of Santa Claus in Harlem would help overcome resistance to its being a rap record. Rocky and J.B. wrote most of the lyrics for the first half of the song, laying down the concept of the record, and then Kurtis came in to put in the call-and-response rhymes he'd been using uptown, and some that Joey had been using when he performed as the "son of Kurtis Blow."

Looking back, it's a funny thing how naive I was. I trusted Rocky and J.B. completely. I had so little knowledge about contracts and the business that they could have totally ripped us off. We signed contracts with them without consulting a lawyer because we believed they were honest. It was a mistake, one that young people make all the time in this business. We were just lucky that we got in with two honest guys. It didn't have to be that way.

It was sad what happened to most of the old school. As early as 1984, when Kurtis had made a couple of albums, most other original rappers had only cut some 12-inches; it was clear those guys were making no money and were going to make no money. None of these guys had professional managers. Their business was being handled by relatives, friends or small-time gangsters with big-time talk but no knowledge. Unlike Kurtis, who was on a major label, all of them were on small labels that, at best, gave a modest advance and paid little or no royalties. These other rappers would come up to Kurtis's apartment in the Bronx and act like he was living in a mansion, since most of them were still living in the projects or with their moms. Of the old-school originators, I believe Kurtis, between his record sales and the tours we'd get him on, was the only one making a real good living from hip-hop. And the fact that Kurtis did so well is why Rush Management would later grow so large. But first we had to get our record made—and that wasn't easy.

"WE'RE STILL GONNA GO TO THE MOON"

I'll never forget this: It was fall 1979 and there was a show at the Armory in Queens. There were probably four thousand kids there. Hollywood was there, as were most of the performers now known as the old school   Flash, the Furious Five, Cheeba and others. A DJ played "Rapper's Delight" by the Sugarhill Gang. It was the first time most of us had heard the record, and we were just stunned. Someone had taken our rhymes, our attitude and our culture and made a record. And not one of us in the community had anything to do with it! I remember after the record played,

DJ Starski got on the mike and said, "Y'all know we started this shit. Don't worry. We're still gonna go to the moon."

All of us—MCs, DJs, promoters—resented it. I personally was wrecked. I had so much animosity toward the Sugarhill Gang. They sure weren't known where the real MCs hung out. At a place like the Disco Fever, a hip-hop hangout in the Bronx, I felt they'd get booed just walking in the door. A few people thought, "Well, that's it. The one rap record that's ever going to be on the radio is out, and none of us made it." Rocky, J.B. and I had been having no luck getting anyone interested in financing or releasing a Kurtis Blow record. So hearing "Rapper's Delight" was deeply disappointing. You see, at first we thought that record had shut the door, when in reality that door was about to swing wide open.

After the Sugarhill Gang record came out, Rocky, J.B. and I focused on getting "Christmas Rappin'" finished and sold. Through Rocky and J.B. I fell in with a group of musicians from Queens, real jazzy types who'd work with us for the next few years—Denzel Miller, a keyboardist, guitarist Eddie Martinez (who later played on "Rock Box"), drummer Trevor Gale and a bass player named Larry Smith, who'd become my producing partner. Most of these guys were jazz players turned R&B heads, and you can hear their influence in all the early Kurtis Blow records.

We recorded at Greene Street studio with an engineer named Rodney Hui, who would be behind the board for many early rap hits. Working on "Christmas Rappin'" was my first time in the studio, but I was never passive. I had suggestions about how the beat should feel and on the melody and the rhymes. But Rocky and J.B. ran the sessions and took Kurtis in a more R&B direction, with strong hooks and choruses that made "Christmas Rappin'" and later "The Breaks" very radio-friendly. They were great records, but I knew they didn't truly reflect the hard-core b-boy attitude in the street.

Once we'd finished "Christmas Rappin'," we began shopping it around town. There was interest, but no one was biting. The industry's attitude was that "Rapper's Delight," despite its U.S. sales and international appeal (it went top ten all over the world), was an unrepeatable fluke. We identified PolyGram, which had a great roster of funk and R&B acts (Kool & the Gang, the Gap Band, Parliament), as the best place for Kurtis, so we made up a gang of test pressings and took them to clubs all over the city. Response in the street from DJs and club goers was great. So to hype up PolyGram we placed fake orders for the record in their system by telling retailers and wholesalers to order the 12-inch through PolyGram. PolyGram didn't own it yet, but we created an appetite for "Christmas Rappin'" that led them to buy it.

Significantly, the 12-inch wasn't picked up by the black music department. A white English A&R guy made the deal. The black music executives reluctantly promoted it as a novelty record, nothing more. That a white man would give hip-hop a chance and black adults established in the business were skeptical was typical of rap's ongoing struggle for credibility with black industry executives.

So in the fall of 1979 Kurtis Blow signed with Mercury Records, a division of PolyGram, making him the first rapper on a major label. Christmas Eve 1979 was the first time I heard "Christmas Rappin'" on the radio; I was upstairs at my family's house. Frankie Crocker, the biggest radio DJ in New York, played it on WBLS.

I ran downstairs. I told my mother. I told my father. I sat looking at the speakers. A record I made was on the radio. It was an unbelievable moment.

Unfortunately, that was one of the only times 'BLS played the record. Like I said, most people saw it as a novelty. But the limited airplay "Christmas Rappin'" received at 'BLS and other urban stations at the end of '79 was the crack we needed. Over the course of the next seven months Kurtis and I traveled all over the country, as well as overseas, based on that one record. Though it was a holiday record, "Christmas Rappin'" played on black radio stations and in clubs around the country well into the summer of '80. We went down to places like South Carolina to work gigs in July and August because "Christmas Rappin'" was just breaking in many markets.

That was an amazing time for me. Everything was new, and it was the first time I had ever really felt successful. I remember in early 1980 I'd been sniffing coke all night when Kurt and I got a call at nine o'clock in the morning. It was Rocky. "You're going to Amsterdam," he said. I'd only been on one plane in my life—a short trip to Philly when I was a kid. Now I was so large I needed a passport because I was going to Europe.

We got to Amsterdam, and immediately the local record company rep took us to a weed house. The whole time we were just waiting to be raided. Then we came out of the weed house paranoid, expecting to be arrested. Then we thought we were being followed back to the hotel. After a while we realized that nothing was going to happen. Not only was weed legal in Amsterdam, but in fact everyone in town seemed happy we were there. So, of course, once we realized that, we went back to the weed house. Here we were, two students from City College, being flown to another country for Kurtis to perform a hit record. I felt rich. That shit felt amazing!

SUGAR HILL

The first institution in hip-hop was Sugar Hill Records, a black-owned label out of Englewood, New Jersey. Sylvia Robinson had been a minor R&B star in the '70s ("Pillow Talk"), and she and her husband, Joe, had run a really ghetto R&B label called All Platinum that went bankrupt. Their most popular act had been a falsetto-lead vocal group, the Moments, who had a string of hits ("Love on a Two-Way Street" was the biggest) and later changed their name to Ray, Goodman & Brown. They jumped on hip-hop to get back in business, and they were the first people to make any real money in the game.

Soon after they put out "Rapper's Delight" they signed up real MCs like Spoonie Gee, Busy Bee, the Treacherous Three (Kool Moe Dee was a member) and, most important, Grandmaster Flash & the Furious Five, who'd become the first successful old-school group to blow up nationally. In fact, Flash & the Five would, with "The Message" and "The Adventures of Grandmaster Flash on the Wheels of Steel," make hip-hop's first artistically important records.

Sylvia Robinson was like everybody's mother. You'd often see her in an uptown club sitting at the bar, looking like royalty. She was always very nice to me, and her son Joey was always cool to me. I wasn't really a competitor, because they were making a lot of money and at the time I was just some young guy managing some acts. To this day I never felt any threat or negativity from them. The only difference between me and Sugar Hill is that I got my artists paid more than Sugar Hill would pay.

As a manager, I never handled a Sugar Hill act. I never even went in their building out in Englewood. It was never like, "Oh, I'm Flash's manager. How come he didn't get a royalty check?" So I guess that's why they never bothered me. It just happened to work out that way. I loved Flash—that's my man forever and ever—but he and his crew never had a manager once they started making records. In fact, I don't think anybody at Sugar Hill had a manager once they started making records there. I don't think Busy Bee or the Treacherous Three or Spoonie Gee or any of them had a manager. Sugar Hill should have been as successful and enduring a label as Def Jam, but they weren't able to build on that early monopoly position. As more labels moved into the rap game, Sugar Hill's deals looked less attractive, and the newer talent signed on elsewhere. You have to stay competitive. The basic truth about the record business is this: You get ripped off, and then you learn to rip the next person off. That's how I've seen it work. Now, I was never jerked by the people who first brought me into the record game. Rocky and J.B. didn't jerk me, so I don't jerk people. I know that sounds simplistic, but then the truth is always very simple. It's lying that's tricky. So treating people fairly is one reason I'm still here and so many of my former competitors are not.

I did a radio interview a couple of years ago in Los Angeles along with Snoop Dogg and the Dogg Pound. I told the interviewer that I'd given Kurtis Blow ten points on his records, and Snoop Dogg almost fell out of his seat. Royalty points are the cream in a recording act's coffee. The more points you have, the more money you make on record sales. Out of a universe of a hundred points, most artists get less than ten points on average. We'd given Kurtis ten points, which was what we could afford back then, and Snoop was shocked. My impression was that his early deals weren't very generous.

But to be fair to Sugar Hill, it's hard to be really generous with points and payments as an independent label. If you have less, you generally give less. Your pockets aren't as deep as Sony's or BMG's. Often you survive from record to record. But if you start doing well and come to dominate the market, as Sugar Hill did in the early '80s, then you should share the wealth. If you expand the market, as Sugar Hill did, you encourage others to enter the business, which is what began to happen. Once that happens, paying the market rate is the only way to hold on to your artists and stay competitive.

MAKING CONVERTS

In 1981 I was 24 years old and feeling a lot of pressure. Here I was with Kurtis Blow, an act that had two gold singles ("Christmas Rappin'" and "The Breaks") and who was getting booked on major tours. In the wake of that success my management company was signing new clients every week, as more rappers were recording and needed representation. At that time there were no other managers who knew or cared about hip-hop with any credibility in that community. And on top of that, I was producing records, too.

Yet I didn't really know how to do some of the things I had to. Everything was new, and there was no textbook. I was learning how to be a manager with every meeting, with every phone call. Often it was just a matter of learning to command respect, which comes with the confidence that you know what you're talking about.

The biggest challenge was dealing with concert promoters. In 1982, following on the success of Kurtis Blow's "The Breaks," we were booked by the major urban promoters of the time—Al Hayman and Quenton Perry. Because we were hot and simple to book (just a DJ, an MC and a road manager), that year Kurtis Blow opened a tour for the Commodores, who were a huge act before Lionel Richie went solo. From that tour we got great exposure and were well paid. In contrast, when we booked Kurtis as a solo act, we dealt with low-level promoters who wouldn't pay you until after the show—if you could find them after the gig. When we were on tour with the Commodores, we had to promote our album on the club circuit. Kurtis and I would roll into a town and he would do radio and in-store appearances to create excitement. We were playing small places and dealing with small-time promoters with short money. Often we'd get beat. We'd be in the dressing room before the show when the promoters would walk in. Either they'd say the gate wasn't as big as they'd hoped or we hadn't done enough promotion or some other bullshit in an attempt to pay us less than we'd contracted for. So we'd be stuck: There'd be a roomful of fans waiting on us—people we needed to go buy the album—and we weren't going to be paid what we'd been promised. Kurtis could have refused go on, but disappointed fans don't buy albums.

A lot of the promoters felt comfortable jerking us because they were sure we were gonna disappear. They just knew Kurtis and I were never gonna come back to their town, so fuck us. Moreover, there was a lot of resentment from traditional promoters and acts about how we performed and the financial advantages it gave us. This was the early '80s. Big bands with horn sections and background singers were the norm in black music. Guys were on the road with seven or eight pieces, plus the roadies and a road manager. They'd all walk away with $10 per gig, while Kurtis, with a DJ and a road manager, was making less but pocketing more. There was no big nightly nut to crack for a rap act. We were revolutionizing the concert business by playing major venues without a band. People acted like we were stealing money, so they treated us like thieves.

Because Kurtis's act was so simple production-wise, we could do incredible things. For example, there was one day that Kurtis played in three different fifteen-thousand-seat arenas in three cities. First we were in Birmingham, Alabama, with Graham Central Station and the Bar-Kays. Then we flew to Greensboro, North Carolina, and opened for the Commodores, Patti LaBelle, and Stephanie Mills. Then we hopped another plane to Augusta, Georgia, where we closed for Con Funk Shun and Cameo.

Cameo was a hell of an act to come behind, especially at that stage of their career. Those guys were a loud, flashy funk band that really put on a show. But Davey D would just go out there and tear shit up on the turntables, and then Kurtis would come on and rock the house. You gotta remember that in a lot of these markets this was the first time people were seeing hip-hop. We'd be up there setting up turntables on the stage and people in the crowd would mutter, "We paid money to see a band." But night after night people would be up dancing on their seats by the end of the set.

I remember our booking agent, a real character named Norby Walters, who worked with us for years and still didn't understand what we did. Norby was a real old-school hustler who had specialized in lounge acts until disco came in. When disco came in, he got his lounge singers to tour as disco acts. From that he got into black music and for a long time had the biggest booking agency in the game. But his company had been booking us for a while before he actually saw what we did. So when he came to San Diego one time to see our show, he just stood there with his mouth open as the crowd went crazy. Norby had seen a lot of things, but never two turntables and a microphone wreck a packed arena. As Flavor Flav said later, "We got some nonbelievers out here tonight." But everywhere we went we made converts.

5 DJ RUN/ DISCO SON

Run-D.M.C. is the most important act in hip-hop history, and I'm proud to say their story began in my family's attic. When my older brother, Danny, moved out of the house, my little brother, Joey, and I used the attic as a recreation room. Joey was always interested in music, so when he was 10 my father bought him a drum set and our neighbor Gpuddy gave him some lessons.

By 12 Joey had moved on to working turntables. Looking back, I can see that with the rise of disco, kids coming up all over the country were setting aside instruments for the ones and twos of the turntables. He was part of a whole generational shift that was happening in how kids related to music. No longer would learning instruments be the only way or even the best way to build a career in music. With knowledge of two turntables, a mixing board, a microphone, a beat box and some appreciation for echo chambers, you too could end up on the cover of *Rolling Stone*. Because of the massive success of his rap band, Run would eventually be one of the leaders in changing how people thought about music. We were a creative family, so it didn't take long for him to figure DJing out. He'd be up in the attic cutting on the wheels of steel, and everybody who heard him knew immediately he was gifted. Now, DJ Hollywood had a "disco son" in DJ Small. Since Kurtis Blow was looking up to Hollywood, he too had to have a disco son—a protégé who played turntables—and that became my brother Joey, aka DJ Run. Kurtis used to rhyme in his stage show, "Fast as an exploding bullet from a gun / is my disco son / Run."

Joey learned the rap game quickly and began writing rhymes, many of which Kurtis used. For example, DJ Run wrote, "I'm DJ Run on the microphone and a place called Krypton was my home," which is in the second half of Kurtis Blow's "Christmas Rappin'" with Kurtis's name in Run's spot. Kurtis is still getting checks from Run's rhymes, but back then everybody used everybody else's rhymes, so it didn't matter.

The thing about Run as a DJ was that he was able to "cut air" on the turntables, which means he could cut the record so fast you wouldn't hear anything but the cracking of the vinyl. That's how quick he could cut. After he broke his arm, Run learned to DJ with one arm. Eventually going to school and DJing with one arm caught up to him, and Davey D took his job with Kurtis. But that was all right because in his heart Run was always a rapper, and at age 17, his last year in high school, I put him in the studio with two friends and he started making records.

One friend, Darryl McDaniel, aka D.M.C., had gone to public school with Run, and they'd known each other all their lives. Like Run, he came up with hip-hop and his taste was totally street. He had zero tolerance for R&B. I remember before Run-D.M.C. started recording we played Kurtis's "Starlife" for him, which was a real R&B-sounding rap record with girl singers and a bright, upbeat arrangement. D.M.C. was like, "Uh-uh, y'all are finished." And to a great degree he was right. The kind of records Kurtis was making would be made obsolete by Run and D.M.C. Radio-friendly rap would never disappear, but there was a clear line already developing between the softer and harder sides of the culture.

The group's third member, Jason Mizell, aka Jam Master Jay, was from Hollis. He'd known Run and D.M.C. for years, but Jay was more street than the other two. Joey had some street in him. D.M.C. didn't. He was pure MC. When they used to play in parks around the way, it was Jay who had the equipment.

One of the things that distinguished them from other young rap crews is that they had lots of routines, series of rhymes they threw back and forth between the two of them like their heroes, the Cold Crush Brothers from the Bronx. You can hear many of the routines on Run-D.M.C.'s early records. The original lyric to "Sucker MCs" came from a routine: "The chauffeur drove off and never came back / went uptown to buy some black / the shit was not the wack / So I got a nickel / picked up the phone / drove off in a Caddy with a light green tone." Another famous record, "Here We Go," wasn't just some rhymes—it came from a routine: "Dum-diddy-dum, diddy-diddy-dum-dum / Cool chief rocker / don't drink vodka / keep a bag of cheeba inside my locker."

It's too bad that when Cold Crush had a chance to make a record in the early '80s, they went away from their strength. It was like they said, "Instead of doing what we do live, we're gonna make a record. We want something bigger." They should have stuck to what had made them special. Run-D.M.C.'s greatest asset was that they never aspired to be bigger. They aspired to keep it real when that wasn't yet considered important in rap. And that attitude allowed them to outdistance all other rappers in the '80s.

"SUCKER MCS"

Larry Smith and I had been junior partners in making the Kurtis Blow records. We had input, but Rocky, J.B. and even Kurtis had a lot more to say than we did. With Run-D.M.C., we got our chance to go in a direction that truly reflected the b-boy attitude. With the 12-inch "It's Like That" b/w "Sucker MCs" we became real producers and, I believe, revolutionized the sound of hip-hop records. At that point in my life I hated R&B and I hated melody. Those first Run-D.M.C. records totally reflect where I was at the time.

"It's Like That" was really Larry's track. We'd listened to Bambaataa's "Planet Rock" and decided we wanted to make a record with that vibe. Our challenge was to take the Bambaataa concept and adapt it. The ironic thing is that back then we'd go in the studio trying to rip off a specific record and when we were finished, no one could tell what record had influenced us. We'd think we were remaking "Apache" by the Incredible Bongo Band and we'd play our record for people and they'd say, "Where's 'Apache'?" I remember giving Bambaataa a copy of "It's Like That" in the Roxy roller rink and telling him, "It's a lot like your record 'Planet Rock.'" Bambaataa played it and then he looked at me like I was crazy.

As a producer, when I made records I'd think it was obvious

what other records influenced me. But when I was finished they didn't sound like any other records out there. Everything Larry, Run, Dee, Jay or myself made during that period sounded unique. That is a rare thing and, looking back at it, quite amazing. Because of the way it sounded and the impact it had on how people heard rap records, I believe coproducing "Sucker MCs" is the single most creative thing I've ever done. The drum beat on that record is mine, and it's been bitten countless times since we laid it down. It was one of the first original b-boy break beats made for a rap record.

PROFILIN'

After we'd cut Run-D.M.C.'s records, I signed Run-D.M.C. to the independent label Profile records. It was 1983. At that time there was no major label supporting rap—Kurtis was on Mercury struggling for attention despite his hits—so we got the best deal we could. Profile was the best independent label at the time, which meant they might pay you a little bit instead of nothing at all. We signed a contract for ten points and an advance of $25,000 for the first Run-D.M.C. album. We spent $15,000 recording the album and split the remaining $10,000 between Larry, Run, Dee and myself. On the second album Jay got down as a full member of Run-D.M.C.

To radio programmers, "Sucker MCs" was the absolute worst record on the radio in years. No one could even imagine what the fuck it was. No melody. No harmony. No keyboards. Just a beat, some fake-sounding hand claps and these niggas from Queens yelling over the track. For that record to be a hit on the radio baffled all the people whose job it was to know what good music is.

"It's Like That" and "Sucker MCs" made Run-D.M.C.'s self-titled debut the first gold rap album. Later we had records that sold more, but that first album is still a classic. That's because it was a collection of singles. When you're making a single, you focus all your energy into making the greatest record you possibly can, since that's all you're working on. "Hard Times," "Jam-Master Jay," "It's Like That," "Sucker MCs," and "Rock Box" were all out in the marketplace before the album dropped. So we had five hot records out before the album actually hit the market.

"Rock Box" was what got us on MTV. It had a loud guitar played by Eddie Martinez anchoring the track, giving it rock credibility. The video had the then-popular comic Professor Irwin Corey in it for comic relief and a little white kid in it for white people to identify with, and we shot it at the hottest punk rock club of that time, Danceteria. The video was our vehicle to get our song out to a mass audience. But the song was as honest as hell—it was no sellout. I knew that there was a kinship between the more rebellious aspects of rock and what was developing in hip-hop. Run-D.M.C. tapped into an edge of teenage anger that for years had been associated with loud, yelling rock singers. The rock-rap linkages that everyone takes for granted now could be heard even back then in the parks when DJs cut up Billy Squier's "The Big Beat" and Aerosmith's "Walk This Way."

Run-D.M.C.'s second album was not as good as the first. It had a few good tracks: "King of Rock," which is as good as anything they've ever done, and "You're Blind." But overall it was made too quickly and lacked the same emphasis on sounding unique that the first album had. A lot of the problem was economic: We had to deliver the second album to Profile in order to get paid for the first.

Despite some tension in our relationship with Profile over money, they had an excellent radio promotion guy in Manny Bella, and they spent money to go after radio programmers to pay attention to their records, which is one of the reasons they were better than other independent labels. And they spent some money on marketing (snipes, giveaways), so I can't say they were cheap. But the reason Run-D.M.C. succeeded was that those three had the will to live. They had amazing endurance because throughout the '80s they watched other groups—lesser groups—get signed to major labels and get paid, while they never got a huge check even though they were rap's biggest band. Profile never gave them the kind of points or up-front advances other bands of their stature got.

Run-D.M.C. eventually made their money on the road. At their peak they were getting up to $100,000 a night, so they just kept touring. After we had a hit with "My Adidas," we negotiated with that German athletic wear company to give us a deal—at one point it was $1 million a year for three years. So they had very significant income outside Profile that kept them going. In a way records were their calling card, while Run-D.M.C. paid their bills through these other activities.

OUTSIDE THE BUILDING

Starting out, I always wanted to be in the building inside one of the big labels. During the early days of Blow and Run I used to do club promotion for PolyGram. Basically I took records around to local club DJs, talked shit and got them high. But it allowed me to meet a lot of the executives at the label. They had nice offices, gold records on the wall and fat expense accounts. To a kid who a year or two before had been selling fake cocaine, working at a label looked great. But the people in the black music department looked at me—scruffy beard, Adidas sneakers, track suit, ghetto music—and didn't see me as corporate material.

Turned out I was lucky that they wouldn't let me in, 'cause everything worth knowing in this business happens outside the building. Eventually I got to know everybody who was a player, because once I had a hot record they had to call me. No one cared who I was, what I wore or even what my records sounded like if I had something they wanted. So a hot record was the best calling card I could have.

I learned there is a cycle to a hit record: The booking agencies and the concert promoters call to book you. Once on the road, you meet all the record retailers and learn their business when your act stops by to sign autographs. When the act does radio interviews in cities they perform in, you meet all the radio programmers. So on tour you learn retail, radio, marketing and promotion. And, of course, all this information helps you grow as a manager.

All that stuff can't be learned inside a building, because when you work at a label you can only do one job at a time. The 1984 Fresh Fest tour was a triumph of being locked outside the building. It was a tour that put the boot to the ground for rap. Fans flocked to those concerts because of hit records. They saw Run-D.M.C., Whodini, Kurtis Blow and the Fat Boys, as well as DJs and break-dancers. When they left they were not only buyers of records and concert tickets, but fans of the culture.

Until the Fresh Fest no one could have imagined an entire tour of music acts and not one band. We sure never imagined it. Then a black promoter named Ricky Walker called us and booked Run-D.M.C. to headline the tour for $5,000 a night. Whodini, Kurtis Blow and the Fat Boys got $3,500 per show. I managed all of the acts except the Fat Boys, and Kurtis Blow produced them. So Rush Management was commissioning about $1,200 or something a show. I thought I was rich. Fresh Fest went to fifty markets and made around $3.5 million, which amazed the entire industry.

It was on the Fresh Fest tour that Run-D.M.C. established their reputation as entertainers. They'd been onstage many times with Kurtis Blow before making records and had always been great. They were b-boys beyond belief. They wore sneakers when other rappers were rocking thigh-high boots like Rick James. They wore leather suits and hats when other rappers had on cowboy outfits, feathers and studded jackets like heavy metal stars. Because ghetto shit came as second nature to many of the early MCs, they didn't see the theatrics in their own lives. They'd polish it up for mass consumption by wearing what Rick James or a rock band would wear. Run-D.M.C. saw what was happening in the street and stayed true to it. I've always thought it takes a bit of a suburbanite—as we were, coming from Queens—to see the power in ghetto culture.

Rick Rubin, who would later become my partner at Def Jam, used to say, "Create the drama to make the theatrics." At that point

Rick was so suburban he would equate the promotion of rappers with wrestling—and this was twenty years before the WWF blew up. What Rick saw was that rappers, just like wrestlers, took basic young male fantasies of power and inflated them into larger-than-life, over-the-top cartoons. For the kids who couldn't be super-strong or really hard-core, rappers and wrestlers acted out their fantasies for them. Some of the artists back then looked at rap as such a ghetto phenomenon that they felt the need to tone it down and make it slicker for the masses. What Rick and I preached was "Fuck being acceptable! Take that ghetto attitude and shove it down their throat." Flash and the others were trying to appeal to a bigger audience, whereas Run-D.M.C. was appealing to a smaller audience; because of that, Run-D.M.C. became the bigger act. It sounds crazy, but that's how it works. Catering to a mass audience usually backfires. Instead the key thing is to stay in your lane, and if you are good enough and interesting enough, people move to you. That way you change the mainstream, and that's what Run-D.M.C. did, opening the door for the rest of the acts and culture to continue that process.

Run-D.M.C. wore Hollis Avenue suits right out of Brooklyn and Queens. Leather suits with velour hats and shell-toe Adidas shoes—that's a ghetto uniform, not a costume. Flash and the Furious Five wore Rick James outfits trying to be rock stars. Run-D.M.C., precisely because of their indifference toward the rock audience, became rock stars. You also have to remember the state of black music in the mid-'80s. Everybody was talking about crossing over to the pop audience. Michael Jackson, Lionel Richie, Luther Vandross and Freddie Jackson, with their soft, unaggressive music (and nonthreatening images), constituted the black music mainstream. So the first chance I got, I did exactly the opposite. B-boys liked music that was spare. So I made the sparest records. B-boys liked loud drums, so I made the loudest drums. On the whole first two albums we didn't use any sounds that were anything like the R&B records that were out.

If you listen to Run-D.M.C.'s "It's Like That" and "Hard Times," you'll find what we used for melody was implied melody, and what we used for music was sounds—beats, scratches, stuff played backward, nothing pretty or sweet. Listen to the song "Thirty Days" right now and you wonder, "What the fuck were they trying to do?" Listen to "Darryl and Joe" and, again, it's all sounds but no music, no real melody. Larry Smith, who made all the early Run-D.M.C. records with me, was an R&B person; he played and wrote a lot of Kurtis Blow material. We'd sit around all day talking about creating a Run-D.M.C. sound, and I'd be rejecting all Larry's more R&B-based ideas. We'd discuss making our synthesizer sound like no one else's. There were no programs around that made the sounds we wanted, so we created our own in search of sounds that weren't already on the radio.

Larry had to go over to London to work with Whodini to have the freedom to make music again, because I wouldn't make no fuckin' music for Run-D.M.C. I loved "Freaks Come Out at Night," "Five Minutes of Funk" and the other hits Larry made for Whodini—it was hip-hop for adult black people who hated rap—but that's not what Run-D.M.C. was about. I remember I got so mad when we made "You Talk Too Much" for Run-D.M.C. because Larry snuck a bass line in.

The band didn't need music anyway. Joey created "Peter Piper" with his turntables. Jay made "Jam-Master Jay," which when it came out was the most unusual record in the world. I remember playing "Jam-Master Jay" in Disco Fever at five in the morning. We came out of the studio and went right there and played the record. The MC that night said, "What was that shit?" I told him it was the new Run-D.M.C. record. He replied, "Well, let me know next time you play it, so I'll be prepared for that shit." His anger was understandable, since the sound of the record made him spill all his coke.

Usually when you test a record you hope everybody dances. With this one I stood in the middle of the floor and watched the entire dance floor empty. But I knew it was a hit! Back then I was in my element; even if people raced back to their seats, I could say to myself, "Oh, my God, I got a hit!" I could just feel it and know.

It was really a very experimental time for me musically. I edited "King of Rock" and took the middle of the record and used it as the intro. We'd chop up those tracks in crazy ways. I believe "King of Rock" had something like three hundred edits. We knew when we were making the records that later we'd chop them up. We'd just cut the beats and the rhymes and later arrange them in the edits.

When I hear those early records I'm so happy that they hold up. I heard a Run-D.M.C. record in a store the other day, with Joey and Dee yelling on the track. Yelling is not cool now among rappers (though DMX has brought it back some), but it sounded so good. "Peter Piper" might sound a little old now, but if you'd put out "Beats to the Rhyme" in 2001, it would still play on the radio.

When Run-D.M.C. performed at the 1999 MTV Music

Awards with Kid Rock, all they had to do was go onstage and do the same thing they've been doing for twenty years. Kid Rock was rhyming "King of Rock" because that record, that idea, is still hot. That means Run-D.M.C. is still current. An old record of theirs sounds great right now. That's a good thing. It just shows that if you maintain your honesty and integrity, commercial success and longevity will follow. That's a lesson I could only have learned outside the building.

I BE ILLIN'

As my career took off so did my sex life. I wasn't a player yet, but I'd come a long way from when I lost my virginity to this girl named Joyce. She was the daughter of one of my mother's best friends. She was 12. I was 14. Joyce was fine and sexy, and her favorite record was "Show Me How" by the Emotions. We did it in my family's attic.

My first important love relationship was with a girl nicknamed Puppet, aka Paulette Mims. She and her mother lived on 209th Street, just four blocks from me. I'd known her several years before we started dating. In fact, when I was in the Seven Immortals she was in the gang's female division. Puppet had curly hair and a big butt. What more did a man need? When I was in City College, Puppet was attending Bayside High. From my college years till I was about 24, Puppet was my ace.

I mean, I slept with other people during that time, but she was my girl for real. So much so that when I got my first check for "Christmas Rappin'" I moved out of my parents' house and bought a home in Brooklyn, and Puppet moved in with me. The place was right across from the Albany projects in Bedford-Stuyvesant. I knew it wasn't the best real estate purchase when crackheads started knocking on my door asking if I wanted a hit—and I did! That attempt at domesticity didn't last very long. With my record career taking off, my mind wasn't focused on being a good boyfriend. When I moved out I left the place to Puppet. That event corresponded with the release of Run-D.M.C.'s "Rock Box" and the beginning of a very busy, wandering, ultradecadent period. First I lived with Andre Harrell out in the huge Lefrak City housing complex in Queens. Andre was living a double life at the time—by day he sold radio spots for a local station and by night he was a member of the rap duo Dr. Jeckyll & Mr. Hyde. Andre and his partner Alonzo Brown were the first (and remain the only) act in hip-hop history to perform in suits and ties, which may account for their average record sales.

It was like the Odd Couple in his place, since Andre was a very upwardly mobile, suit-and-tie-wearing black man and I was really starting to get into an edgy, hip-hop-meets-punk-rock lifestyle. Here's an example of the difference: One Friday night we were both in the elevator going out on dates. He was in a three-piece suit with his lawyer girlfriend going to play miniature golf. I was with an English punk rock white girl, going to see Suicidal Tendencies and the Dead Kennedys.

I woke up the next morning at the girl's place and witnessed her and a 60-year-old punk rock woman free-basing. It was the first time I'd ever seen free-basing or smelled coke cooked up like that. Waking up as I did, seeing them do this weird shit, for a minute I thought I was in hell. Of course it only made me wanna see this girl more. We developed a great relationship. We'd fuck anywhere anytime. We fucked in many restrooms and a couple of times on the street. Eventually she moved to England and I'd see her every time I went there.

Next I roomed for a while with Lyor Cohen, who was working at Rush Management at that time, helping us with bookings and the day-to-day hand holding you have to do with acts. Then I decided to turn a part of the Rush office on lower Park Avenue into an apartment and move in. This was very convenient for me but not so good for some of my employees, since I used to have sex with girls during business hours. That's how I was living.

My next permanent apartment was on LaGuardia Place in the Village. The building was blue with images of flying pigs painted on it. Since the downtown scene was now so much a part of my life, it was a perfect spot. I had a lot of fun there. Not all that play turned out well. I met a cute, brown-skinned girl named Tammi through a friend. Tammi wanted to be in the entertainment business. In the meantime she made money selling coke. I'd stop over at Tammi's to do lines and have sex. It seemed like a good arrangement.

So good she apparently had similar deals with other guys. One Friday night I stopped over about eight for some rest and relaxation. I left around nine. A few days later I received a call from the police. Tammi was dead and a "bald black man fitting my description" had been seen exiting the crime scene. I was interviewed by the district attorney several times before it became clear another man had come to see Tammi after I had and he, not me, was the killer.

That was a real scary experience, but Tammi's death didn't cause me to change my lifestyle. I was young and just coming into money, and there was too much going on for me to stop. It seemed all good.

6 THE DEF YEARS

In 1984 things were going well. Rush Management was the biggest management company in hip-hop. I had Kurtis Blow, Whodini, the Fearless Four and many other acts. I had a hip-hop band called Orange Krush that included Davey DMX, Larry Smith, the drummer Trevor Gale and the singer Alyson Williams, whom I later signed as a solo act. Orange Krush had already made one influential record, "Action," that had one of the best break beats ever. Along with Larry I'd produced the first two Run-D.M.C. albums.

So I was juggling management and production and was enjoying both. One day I heard "It's Yours," a record by T. La Rock & Jazzy J, and I loved it. I noticed that while it was distributed by Street Wise records, it had a little logo on it that read "Def Jam." One night at a club DJ Jazzy J came over and asked me if I wanted to meet the man who'd made "It's Yours." Jazzy J walked me over to this stocky, long-haired Long Island white kid. I was surprised that this was the man behind Def Jam, but after we started talking I realized that Rick Rubin and I had a lot in common. His musical and cultural interests were the same as mine. Plus he had a real understated sense of humor that I enjoyed and which was often reflected in his records. So we began to hang. He told me that aside from being into hip-hop he was also a member of a punk rock band and on top of that was running his new little label, Def Jam, out of his NYU dorm on University Place in the Village.

Rick was an unlikely-looking guy to be involved in making black uptown teenage music. But if you listened to the production of "It's Yours," it was clear that Rick really understood the aesthetic: big, huge beats, minimal melody and aggressive vocals. When I started hanging out with him and watching him work drum machines, there was no question Rick was a beat-making motherfucker. And we had chemistry. We both hated the soft-ass black music that was on the radio; we both enjoyed the rebel attitude that hip-hop embodied; we both saw that there was more in common between AC/DC and rappers than between rappers and Luther Vandross. When Rick told me his inspiration for wanting to make rap records was "Rock Box," it made perfect sense. We made a good team—I was a manager/producer type, and Rick made beats and understood the attitude.

Rick came into the studio and coproduced Run-D.M.C.'s third album, *Raising Hell,* with me. Run-D.M.C. itself conceived and produced the album's first single, "Peter Piper," on which Jam Master Jay cut up Bob James's "Mardi Gras," while Run and D traded rhymes. The three of them could make records like that all day. But when we decided to make a rock record, neither Run nor I remembered the name of the band or even the song we wanted to bite. We kept saying we wanted to bite *Toys in the Attic,* which was the name of the album the song was on. Rick told us, "That band is Aerosmith and that song is 'Walk This Way.' They're my heroes. We're gonna call them up and get them in the studio." He had a background in rock and roll that we didn't. He took our idea of using a beat and guitars beyond where we would have on our own. At that time Aerosmith was at a low ebb in their career while Run-D.M.C. was on the rise. So Steve Tyler and the band were very cooperative and we all had a good time together. But did any of us see that this would be a landmark record? No. Much talked about? Yes. A massive hit? Only in our dreams. But it went on to become the biggest single on the album and the song that would resurrect Aerosmith's career.

Rick also had a great sense of style in logos and graphics. The Def Jam logo, one of the best logos in the game, was Rick's work. The funny thing is, he really thought when rappers said "death" (which in the '80s was a slang term of affirmation) that they were saying "def." Black kids may have pronounced it "def," but they would have spelled it *d-e-a-t-h.* They never would have spelled it *d-e-f.* That's the thing about white rock-and-roll or alternative people or suburban people coming into hip-hop culture—their version of the black ghetto is always more dramatic.

That's why Rick only cared about making the records louder. That's what made it exciting to him. Rick was a good example of what people from outside street culture bring to hip-hop. They hear it. They love it. But their point of entry into hip-hop is different, so they manifest it differently. It was like me, the kid from Queens, making the ultimate ghetto b-beat record, "Sucker MC," with no bass line. I came to that record differently than someone from Harlem or the Bronx would have at that time. To me Run-D.M.C. could be both rock and roll and rap, because both were parts of youth culture. It wasn't about race at this level but an energy and attitude that rock and rap shared. Run-D.M.C. did this without being calculated but by being honest about what they liked and wanted to achieve musically. Whether we worked with Larry Smith or Rick Rubin, the band and I weren't concerned with reaching blacks or whites, but with making new sounds for people who wanted to hear them. The long-term effect was that the aggressive style of Run-D.M.C. would ultimately change rock, so that bands like Limp Bizkit and Korn still use the formula we started back in the '80s.

I booked Kurtis Blow in the Mudd Club, the downtown punk hangout, in 1980 because he belonged there. That was a place for new music and other forms of alternative culture (the painter Jean-Michel Basquiat used to hang out there), and Kurtis was new and an alternative to what constituted black pop at the time. The downtown crowd understood that. They hated Lionel Richie and all the crossover black pop as much as, if not more than, we did. Moves like that were the beginnings of globalizing hip-hop culture. What I came to understand was that you've got to think about all the potential audiences that matter but be particularly sensitive to the first audience, the core audience. When I say "core audience" I don't mean that in terms of race but in terms of interest and sensibility. If you never compromise, your core audience will come with you as you grow. Then you build on their loyalty and bring in other people. That's how a great band becomes a hugely popular one.

What I realized in the early '80s was that the people on line outside the club that second day don't mean shit. They'd buy a pet rock. They were on line because they'd heard it was cool from someone who'd been there the first day. It's the first-day audience that's the core—that's who you must be sensitive to. The core hip-hop consumers are active buyers. They know the record's coming. They buy it day one. They talk about it with their friends day one.

And I saw in the early '80s that the core audience for hip-hop was composed of black and white people of many different backgrounds. A great example is Jordan Wald, one of the best A&R men I've ever had at Def Jam. He was the son of the singer Helen Reddy and grew up in Malibu. Yet Jordan knew more about every record we'd made than anyone else in the company. I had Jordan do A&R at Def Jam because he was a core consumer and he felt the music with passion.

I remember Jordan liked the rap duo Nice & Smooth, but he'd say, "Why do they have to wear those silly-ass purple jackets?" which in his opinion were uncool. I agreed with him. The purple suits were too ghetto-specific, too R&B-looking (like something a vocal group would wear) and not forward-looking. The purple suit symbolized a style that was popular with only certain aspects of the black community. It was very old-school and very traditional—a soul-era idea of urban flash that didn't have the same edgy youth appeal of hip-hop. Instead we dressed Nice & Smooth in Timberland outfits—clothes that were younger in feel and which both black and white kids thought were cool at the time. That simple change helped get Nice & Smooth on MTV. That's part of the process: tailoring what's commercial about the act for mass consumption without selling them out. Back when many rap groups used to wear rock star outfits, the problem was they'd gone too far. The subtlety is in picking the right outfit. That's where the art is in positioning your act. You could be too R&B; you could be too rock. In either case, the key is to be aware and understanding of the nuances that make the difference. In all my marketing efforts I try whenever possible to address the entire audience. You have to know your core and noncore audiences and understand how to reach both without alienating either. And you simply can't say "black" and "crossover" because it's more complex than that.

White people might buy 80 percent of hip-hop records today, but I don't think they're as big a percentage of the tastemaking crowd. If you get an underground record that's really cool and innovative, the initial audience might be 40 percent white. There's also a diverse group of black people who are part of that audience, including black people who are not from the same background as the obvious ghetto one. The key is that all of these different groups make up the core tastemaking crowd.

I meet with consultants and they give me research findings that say exactly what I've known since at least 1983—urban street culture is the most trend-setting community in America. The streets reaffirmed Polo. They gave Versace a new audience. They made

RUSSELL SIMMONS

Selling crack in front of our house in Hollis, Queens—that cap may one day make Phat Farm's fall collection.

FUSSELL SIMMONS

PUBLIC SCHOOL
194
QUEENS
1965
CLASS 2-209

Already in 1965, you can see white kids are rare in Hollis—this photo was taken just before I started losing my hair.

GLEN E. FRIEDMAN

Robert "Rocky" Ford helped get me in the music game and, just as important, treated me fairly—a lesson I haven't forgotten.

DAVID SALIDOR

912

This was during Run-D.M.C.'s early years at Profile—judging by my sweater, probably around 1984. That's D.M.C., me, Jam Master Jay, and Profile's owners, Steve Plotnick and Corey Robbins.

RUSSELL SIMMONS

An unprecedented gathering of the old school at lunch preceding the 2001 Hip-Hop Summit. *Standing:* **Grandmaster Flash, Eddie Cheeba, DST, Bam Bam, The Original DJ Hollywood, Sal Abottiello (of Disco Fever), Davy D., and Fly Ty (CEO of Cold Chillin' Records).** *Seated:* **Kurtis Blow, me, and Grandmaster Caz.**

POLYGRAM RECORDS, INC.

3.

"The Breaks," which preceded Kurtis' debut, self-titled LP, made history by garnering a gold 12" from the R.I.A.A. It was the first time a male solo artist had ever earned a gold disc for a 12" record and it catapulted Kurtis' subsequent album onto the R&B, disco and pop charts. Under the direction of his manager, Russell Simmons, Kurtis' career was skyrocketing.

In trying to explain rap to the masses, Mercury made a promotion cartoon of Kurtis Blow. KB looks good, but look what they did to me.

BILL ADLER ARCHIVES

Def Jam recordings

Our Artists Speak For Themselves ('Cause They Can't Sing.)

Even Def Jam's ads back in the day had attitude.

TALIB HAQQ

This was taken in 1983, when all the drugs and alcohol I'd taken had me looking older than I am now.

RUSH MANAGEMENT

DMC   JAM MASTER JAY   RUN

RUN DMC

1133 Broadway,
N.Y., N.Y. 10010
Suite 907

This is Run-D.M.C.'s first official press photo.

TALIB HAQQ

This is the original Rush Management office at 1133 Broadway in New York City. Standing behind me (*left to right*) are Andrew "Dice" Rhamdanny; Bill Adler; Tony Rome; Twana Carney; Heidi Smith; and Andre Harrell.

RICKY POWELL

Rush Management worked with Jazzy Jeff & the Fresh Prince during the period when they became major record sellers. At the signing was (*left to right*) me; Jeff; Will Smith (aka the Fresh Prince); his long-time manager, James "JL" Lassiter, and my partner, Lyor Cohen.

CHASE ROE

The Beastie Boys and Rick Rubin with my coauthor, Nelson George, backstage at Madison Square Garden after the Beasties had opened for Madonna and been booed by most of the audience. This tour helped establish them as both the most loved and most hated band of the 1900s.

JIM STIENFELDT

Here I am with my brilliant photographer and lifetime friend Glen E. Friedman, at the party for his book *Fuck You Too,* which was the follow-up to his first book, *Fuck You Heroes.* I suggested the title for the second book.

BEASTIE BOYS (fall, 1985)

PHOTOGRAPH: GLEN E. FRIEDMAN

LL COOL J (left) and CUT CREATOR (fall, 1985)

SLICK RICK (fall, 1988)

PHOTOGRAPH: JANETTE BECKMAN

PUBLIC ENEMY (winter, 1987)

DEF JAM CLASSICS, VOL. I

These photos reflect Def Jam's first golden age, when the company blew rap up to a new level of creativity, visibility, and sales.

Here I am outside Def Jam's first office in 1984. You can see how clear-eyed and eager I am.

COURTESY *BLACK ENTERPRISE* MAGAZINE

BLACK ENTERPRISE

BOOK EXCERPT: BECOMING A MANAGER

DECEMBER 1992

B.E. 100s PROFILE

How This 35-Year-Old CEO Built A $34 Million Rap Empire

Special Report:

Are Career Seminars For Black Managers Worth It?

Family Investing For Fun & Profit

$2.50

12

RUSH COMMUNICATIONS CEO
RUSSELL SIMMONS

Making the cover of *Black Enterprise* testified how far rap had come within the African-American community. Even the most conservative elements had to pay attention.

NELSON GEORGE

This photo from 1993 is pretty typical: at a party and on my cell phone, doing business or calling girls.

COURTESY OF HBO

Life-long friend and partner Stan Lathan and that funny nigga Martin Lawrence.

RUSSELL SIMMONS

My mother and me in the early 1990s.

RICEY POWELL

King Ad Rock, me, and supermodel Rachel Williams. As you can tell, I'm twisted off my ass again.

Me and her highness, material girl Madonna, along with my man Guy-O and Mr. Rick Rubin.

RUSSELL SIMMONS

Here I am with Elizabeth Berkeley, Veronica Webb, and "my son," the incredible Brett Ratner, with his two beautiful dates.

RUSSELL SIMMONS

Lyor at a recent party and Reverend Run.

Tommy Hilfiger from scratch. They made beepers part of every-day American life. They made Jeeps cool. They've effected a lot of cultural change. I think the way you prepare your product for that group is crucial.

Everything my companies have done is based in hip-hop culture, whether it is Def Jam, Phat Farm, or *Def Comedy Jam.* It is done with attention to the subtlety of marketing hip-hop on a global scale. I think that's something we've been very good at. My whole career has been about cultivating, understanding and expanding this core audience for hip-hop culture and then watching the impact ripple out to the mainstream.

DEF DAYS

With the platinum sales of Run-D.M.C.'s *King of Rock* on Profile records in 1984, a lot of the majors approached Rick and me about making a distribution deal with Def Jam, which we'd become partners in after he worked with me on Run's album. At the time Rick and I were gonna keep it independent, with our first big release to be an album by this teenage MC from Hollis Rick had signed named L.L. Cool J. But the majors still kept feeling us out for offers. I remember we were flown out to Los Angeles to meet with the president of Warner Bros., Mo Austin, and his staff. At the time Warner Bros. was a market leader and had a reputation as a progressive, artist-friendly company. We walked into a conference room filled with executives. Apparently Mo, who was and is a great guy, wanted his whole staff to be aware of this music coming in from New York.

So we put on L.L. Cool J's "I Need a Beat." The whole room sat there—some of them stared at the speakers, some of them just sat looking at their hands. It was like they were hearing music from another planet. I wasn't offended—it was funny. Rick and I just laughed about it. That afternoon we got the record on KDAY, which had adopted an all-rap format and was breaking records in the L.A. market (Dr. Dre would first come to prominence there doing a mix show). By the time we left town they were playing "I Need a Beat" twelve times a day. Warner Bros., which had always been a solid label, never really caught up to hip-hop, and that's a big reason the label floundered in the '90s.

Eventually, after a lot of meetings, Rick and I finally signed a deal for Def Jam to be distributed by CBS, now Sony, in 1985. That began the next chapter in Def Jam history. We consolidated the offices of Rush Management and Def Jam into a three story building at 398 Elizabeth Street in the Village. Rush Management was on the first floor, Def Jam on the second, Rick lived on the third and a never-completed studio was in the basement. The place was small, cramped and incredibly creative.

In contrast to the sterile, totally out-of-touch atmosphere at a place like Warner Bros., the environment around Def Jam and Rush was creative, supportive and mad open. For example, people will be shocked by this, but it was King Ad-Rock of the Beastie Boys who brought a tape by Todd Smith, aka L.L. Cool J, to Rick Rubin. I don't know precisely how Ad-Rock got it, but he knew immediately that this kid had talent, and of course he was right. It was D.M.C. who first brought Public Enemy to our attention—he knew of them from Roosevelt, Long Island. That's how it worked. Game recognized game, and then Rick and I would move on it.

BUILDING CAREERS

During Def Jam's first golden era, roughly 1986 to 1990, we developed several of the most important acts in hip-hop history— L.L. Cool J, Public Enemy, Slick Rick and the Beastie Boys. Each was different, yet they all shared a vision of pushing the creative envelope while remaining honest to themselves. At the same time Rush Management was involved in breaking Run-D.M.C. for Profile, and Whodini and DJ Jazzy Jeff and the Fresh Prince for Jive.

Just as the Fresh Fest opened the eyes of the country to hip-hop on a national basis, the yearly tours my company, Rush Management, orchestrated throughout the '80s broke acts and continued growing the audience. By the Raising Hell tour in 1986 we were getting 85 percent of the door, which is what the biggest acts get. Run-D.M.C. started making up to $150,000 a night with virtually no production costs. We got what Mick Jagger got, but we never had the overhead the Stones had.

We never formally promoted the tours, but we controlled them. The Raising Hell tour in 1986, the Dope Jam tour in 1987, Together Forever in 1988—we put them together, packaged them and through our booking agents gave promoters in the different regions of the country the rights. So they handled the grunt work— snipes, local promotion, dealing with venue. Sometimes we'd use a national promoter, like Ricky Walker, who'd created the Fresh Fest.

By packing the dates with acts signed to either Rush Management or Def Jam, we developed stars. The opening act—whether it was Slick Rick, the Beasties or Public Enemy—got an opportunity to get visible and make fans. And I'm proud to say all our acts exploited this opportunity well. These signature acts from the Def Jam/Rush Management stable illustrate how rap grew, and today these acts still matter.

L.L. COOL J

Todd was only 16 when we made his first album, *Radio,* so the record is full of his youthful energy and aggressiveness, qualities Rick's stripped-down production of the tracks and vocals really showcased. But there was a more R&B side to him, one Rick really wasn't interested in. I know of a production team from the West Coast called the L.A. Posse—they had an act that I'd passed on, but I liked their tracks. So I hooked them up with L.L. for his second album, *Bigger and Deffer.* He still shouted on that album—as on the hit "I'm Bad"—but the huge success off that album, the single that really widened Todd's audience, was "I Need Love," the first successful rap ballad. I'll never forget the first time Rick heard "I Need Love." It was the worst thing that ever happened in his life. He kept asking, "What are you doing to my son?" Rick just hated it. The truth is, Todd put the same heart into "I Need Love" that he had into "Rock the Bells." I mean, Rick knew it was in L.L., since he'd had two ballads on his debut album, though neither had been singles.

Two days after we released it, "I Need Love" was the number one request on San Francisco's KMEL, which at the time was one of the few all-rap stations in the country. L.L. was just bringing out what was inside him. It wasn't a commercial calculation. It was what he felt. One of the reasons the acts we've worked with at Def Jam stand tall like buildings years after they were first hot is because the foundations were built on honesty. As long as they remain true to themselves, their audience will stay with them and respect them.

As an artist, L.L.'s like Madonna or David Bowie—one of those stars who survive because they can successfully reinvent themselves. His flow has changed five times in the last fifteen years. It's the same L.L., but he always stays contemporary.

The reason for his longevity is that L.L.'s a great writer who can adapt. He can go home to Hollis right now, hang out and find out what niggas are into. He can take that info back to Beverly Hills or a movie set and write a whole album based on the information he's taken in. And he does this while putting his personality into it, so that you can listen to his albums for fifteen years and feel the same consistent point of view despite all the changes in L.L.'s life. That's the honesty and integrity that make him an artist.

L.L. and I have a love/hate relationship. The bottom line is complete love, but we fight over every contract we negotiate. That's because of our familiarity. It's one reason we can argue so passionately. No one's been on Def Jam as long as he has, and despite the sitcoms and the movies he's done, L.L. will always be the king of my label.

PUBLIC ENEMY

Culture is always more important than color in creating and exposing hip-hop. For example, Public Enemy was the most important act in Def Jam history because they epitomized the label's sound and the merger of two cultures—hip-hop and rock. D.M.C. brought a tape to us, and Rick chased them down. The thing no one knows is that Chuck D didn't wanna make records. Rick had to convince them to sign with us, not because there was a bidding war, but because Chuck really wasn't that interested. Think about this: My white, Jewish partner had to convince the most important political rap band of all time to start recording black.

Public Enemy is my favorite Def Jam group, right alongside Jay-Z and DMX, because they made my favorite music. L.L. Cool J's audience may be at one end of the spectrum and the Beastie Boys' audience at the other, but P.E. makes sense to both. P.E. was the most b-boy and the most alternative at the same time. At Def Jam we liked to make records that made people think and that sounded different. That was P.E.

Chuck D was a guy I liked from the first time I met him. I liked his heart and liked his head. He spent all his time looking for new sounds and ways to make old sounds feel new. He was into sonics. It was a point of view similar to what we'd been doing with Run-D.M.C. So Chuck and his crew heard hip-hop just like we did, but they had their own, unique way of getting there.

What made Chuck so great was his ability to hang out with the Beastie Boys while they talked silly shit. He'd hang out with Ice Cube when he was doing his gangsta shit. Yet they'd all come out smarter because of the time they spent with him. He led by example and made people step up their game. Look at Ice Cube's lyrics on the album he made with the Bomb Squad—P.E.'s production crew—compared to what he'd done before and you can feel Chuck's influence.

Chuck got the burden of leadership thrust upon him because of the records he made, and he accepted it. That's a serious decision. He didn't have to do it—he could have just made records. But he went out and talked about shutting down Nike. He said his Uzi weighed a ton. (He was attacked by many Jewish groups.) I've had so many arguments defending Chuck over the years, but I was happy to do it because he had integrity. The band's promotion of Afrocentric ideas led people to pay more attention to Africa, to the Nation of Islam, to Malcolm X—there's no way Spike Lee's movie about Malcolm would have gotten made without the energy they generated around his image and ideas. I often pray for other rap groups to change the game as Public Enemy did.

Now that all that controversy is history, it's easy to see how important Public Enemy was and remains. I don't think it's a stretch to say they were the most important band of their era—rock, rap, R&B, whatever—and remain one of the most influential of all time.

SLICK RICK

I first met Slick Rick at a nuthouse. He'd smoked too much angel dust and had to stay in a mental ward for a few days. Ricky was already famous from his work with Doug E. Fresh on "The Show" and "La-Di-Da-Di." Rick Rubin at Def Jam and Lyor Cohen at Rush Management both thought we should sign him. So I went with Rick to meet him at the hospital. Ricky was completely out of it. I'd seen a lot of people in that dusty state in the street—I'd been that way myself—so I knew that after a few days he'd be fine.

Ricky was one of the most prolific writers and greatest performers at Def Jam. He had a presence that was unreal, more presence than any other rapper, because he had such confidence in himself. He said the most absurd stuff about himself, and he meant it. He could do a silly dance and the audience would love him for it. He'd been in a group called the Kangol Crew and was totally at home in the Kangol cap and in the gold chains that became his signature. Gold was a status symbol, and Rick was a status nigga.

The recording of his classic first album, *The Great Adventures of Slick Rick*, illustrates Ricky's way of doing things. Ricky was too much of an individual to let producers just come in and impose their style on him. Rick Rubin, Larry Smith and many others came in to work with him over the course of a year and a half. But after all that time we only had one usable track—"The Ruler," which was produced by Jam Master Jay. Ricky simply wouldn't rap on tracks he felt no connection to. It had to be organic with him.

So Hank Shocklee and the other Bomb Squad guys came in and really produced with Ricky, helping him fulfill his vision of himself. Within ten days they'd recorded a whole album. And it was the high quality of his music that broke him, though his look certainly didn't hurt. Our video for "Children's Story" by Rick Menello and the album's cover photograph by one of my best friends, Glen Friedman, were both really good depictions of

Ricky's style—the eye patch, the Bally shoes, the chains and the gold teeth. Like all great commercial successes, Ricky took what was going on in the street and put his personal stamp on it.

THE FRESH PRINCE

When Will Smith was still the Fresh Prince and living in Philly he made an indie record that laid out his point of view. On the record Will said, "I got punched in the eye." Someone asked him what he was gonna do. Will's response was, "Hold my eye." Not only was that funny, but it let you know who he was. This wasn't a tough guy. This was just a regular guy like many of us. He got hit, but he wasn't grabbing an Uzi or promising revenge—he was just holding his eye!

I knew that was something that many people would relate to. That's what made me wanna manage him. He had artistic honesty. He was being true to himself. Now that he's a big action star Will would probably hit the guy back, but that attitude of the put-upon man ran through most of his best rap records. His biggest hit as the Fresh Prince, "Parents Just Don't Understand," was just an extension of the boy who held his eye.

THE BEASTIE BOYS

The Beastie Boys are another great example of artistic honesty. When I first saw them live, they were the Young and the Useless, a punk band with more attitude than musicianship. But King Ad-Rock, Mike D and MCA, along with Rick, were always really curious and open. They saw the connection between the downtown music scene they were part of and the uptown music that was growing. When they first started rapping they used to wear red sweat suits with red Pumas to match, trying to look hip-hop. But when I saw them perform as a punk band they wore their natural wardrobe, which was less flashy, yet still loose and cool and hip-hop. In those clothes they were realer. So that became their rap outfit as well. Basically I urged them to be themselves: funny, adventurous natural adapters. I guess it wasn't such a creative bit of management, but sometimes getting an act to be themselves is the toughest thing to do.

The Beasties' first records, "Rock Hard" b/w "She's On It," were steeped in hip-hop. Their record "Hold It, Now Hit It" was what they lived for. It was creative and funny, and pushed the sonic envelope. But the record that blew them up, the record that sent their debut album, *Licensed to Ill,* to four million copies—the most for any rap act up to that point—was a joke to them. They kind of threw "Fight for Your Right" together and didn't care about it. In a way it was a dishonest record—at least they perceived it that way. They felt it pandered to the audience and wasn't quite smart enough to represent what they were really about. Afterward they didn't like performing it when it was huge, and they almost never do it now.

I remember people were amazed to see the Beastie Boys open for Run-D.M.C. on the Raising Hell tour. Was it a risk? No. They had a hit record ("Hold It, Now Hit It") in the street at the time.

They just went out there and did their hot song. The predominantly black audience wasn't racist about it at all. They were like "Yo, that's the white boys." In a pack of acts they stood out. They played in front of black audiences and no one really cared in a negative way. Early in their careers the fact that they were white definitely made them stand out amid Run and P.E. for black audiences. But they were ultimately accepted by black people because they were good.

In fact, the Beasties got way more hostility from the Madonna crowd when they opened for her than from Run's audience. They used to go out in front of Madonna's fans and run around onstage and lip-sync. They'd be joking and falling over while the lip syncing was supposed to be going on. So you'd hear their voices and they'd be laughing. They used to do things like that to irritate that crowd.

They were the band that the MTV audience loved and hated the most. Their videos generated the most letters saying, "Why is this fucking band on TV!" They also had the most letters saying, "This is our favorite band." They got the best fan mail and the worst fan mail at the same time. They were assholes. To some they were the worst fucking group in the world; to others they were the best group in the world. That's a good place to be for a youth band, as long as the people who like you are trendsetters or cultural leaders.

A lot of people were mad at me for managing them, at least at first. I remember there were discussions that the Beasties were a rip-off of black artists. To me the Beasties were honest. They were doing their version of black music. They weren't rip-off artists. They started out halfway trying to be that, but they didn't even know how to do it right. They knew how to do their version of black music, they were creative with it and that's what made it good.

ANDRE UP, LYOR IN

Crucial to the success of Rush Management, the national tours and my overall growth as a businessman was the involvement of Lyor Cohen. A tall, lanky, intense Israeli, Lyor did the detail work on all my management-related business and would grow to be an indispensable part of all my music-related activities. Today he is the president of Def Jam/Island, the most successful label owned by Seagram, and is still involved in all my ventures, from clothing to the Internet to television.

When I first encountered Lyor Cohen in 1983, he was promoting shows at the Hollywood Palladium. He booked Run-D.M.C. on a show with the Red Hot Chili Peppers, the Butthole Surfers and Suicidal Tendencies, so he definitely understood the possibilities of the culture. When he saw Run-D.M.C. in L.A. he fell in love with them.

Not long after that I gave Lyor a small job at Rush Management. He moved to New York, lived in a shitty hotel and was Andre Harrell's assistant. At the time Andre had a new dual life—vice president at Rush while still rapping as Dr. Jeckyll in Dr. Jeckyll & Mr. Hyde. Because Andre was still very involved with his own career, Lyor was handling a lot of business.

One day Andre brought a big, heavyset, light-skinned kid with a bad eye from Mount Vernon, New York, into my office and told me the guy was a sex symbol. I wasn't sure about that. When I heard Heavy D's demo I didn't think he was right for Def Jam. I kept asking Andre, "Why are you playing this R&B for me? What are you trying to do to rap?" Andre believed in Heavy D, who would go on to have several platinum albums, and Andre would eventually get a deal at MCA for his own label, Uptown, where the New Jack Swing sound he promoted there revolutionized R&B.

When Andre left Rush to start Uptown in 1986, Lyor moved up and did a little bit of everything at Rush—road-managed, booked groups, baby-sat. He became the glue that held the management company together, and moved on to guide Def Jam when I got involved in other ventures. He eventually became my chief business partner and one of my greatest, closest friends.

7 HOLLYWOOD 101

In the early '80s Kurtis Blow, Run and a lot of the other artists I managed began expressing interest in acting. There had been a successful but exploitative movie about hip-hop dancers called *Breakin'* that had been shot in L.A., and it looked to us, with all the talent around us, that we should make a movie, too. The problem was, we had no entry to that world.

The only young black man regularly on-screen then was Eddie Murphy, and mostly he was the only black person in his movies. There was no Spike Lee, no John Singleton, no other young black director working at that point. So unlike today, when there are many black directors and stars, the world of filmmaking seemed very far away from us at the time.

Now think about this: The whole idea of a hip-hop movie, for somebody who was greedy, was a way to cash in on a growing trend. However, if you were a serious filmmaker, you wouldn't make a movie about a musical genre. Imagine that kind of mentality: "Oh, yeah, rap is hot. Let's make a movie about rap," without a script, without a concept, with nothing. But eventually that's what happened. People who were entrepreneurs—not creative film people—made a movie with me.

I had a meeting with Menachem Golen and his brother, who'd just made *Breakin'*. I was explaining to him what a rap movie should be about, and they were nodding like they understood all my talk of honesty and artistic integrity. Golen sounded all set to make the movie I wanted to make. I walked out of the meeting and down into the lobby. Right there by the elevators was the late George Jackson, a portly, energetic young black producer, who snatched me and said, "Fuck making a movie with them. You're making a movie with us."

Now, in George's defense I won't say he was just a stupid entrepreneur or just wanted to exploit a culture he knew nothing about. He was black and from the Bronx. But as great a guy as he was, and as much as I loved him, George was still Hollywood. He was running Richard Pryor's film company and hadn't done a movie yet, so he was a hungry, aggressive filmmaker fiending to make a movie.

Anyway, we ended up working with George, and George had to make a lot of promises, because he didn't have the money Menachem Golen had. The Golen brothers ended up making their own movie, a piece of shit called *Rappin'* starring Mario Van Peebles. You heard me—Mario Van Peebles. They didn't know any better.

George had to lie a little bit and hustle a little bit, like filmmakers do, especially if the people you're working with were as stupid as I was at the time. So George said, "We'll do whatever you want." He asked, "Who do you want to direct it?" I didn't know any directors by name, so I said, "What about the guy who made *Cooley High*?" which I had enjoyed. George went and delivered that director, Michael Shultz. Then he told us he had Warner Bros. lined up to distribute the film.

Then, at the last minute, I realized that Warner Bros. wasn't committed at all. I ended up meeting with Mo Austin, head of the record division, because I had a little relationship with him based on that L.L. Cool J meeting. Because Warner Records was gonna get the soundtrack and now understood how big rap was becoming, Mo helped convince the film division to close that deal.

Aside from Mo Austin, another reason the movie *Krush Groove* got made was a story in the *Wall Street Journal* calling me "the mogul of rap." Funniest thing. Rap wasn't shit, but I was the mogul anyway. Anyway, the story came out in advance of getting the financing, and the visibility it gave us definitely helped.

So to be involved in *Krush Groove* I was paid $15,000. Rick Rubin got $15,000 (he also played himself in the movie). Run-D.M.C. jointly got $15,000. Even though George Jackson's the guy who executive-produced the sound track, the cool records on it were all ours. I mean, we gave them a hit sound track. I don't think George made that much, but he made a lot more than me. I guess I have to chalk that one up to experience.

What happened to me at the beginning of my career was a rare thing. Somebody came to me and said, "Never mind your lawyers and the rest. I'm gonna give you a reasonable deal. I'm gonna give you some direction on how you can make some money out of this deal, and I'm gonna support you in the whole process." That's what Robert Ford and J.B. Moore did with me. I learned to do that with other people. I don't expect anybody to ever do that with me again in life. You get what you negotiate. George Jackson and his guys didn't rob me. They gave me associate producer credit and, more important, it was their idea to make the movie about my life as opposed to making it some random rap story.

The fact that Blair Underwood played me was certainly helpful in getting my picture in the black teen magazine *Right On!* The movie got me laid. It helped to get people to recognize what I was doing with Run-D.M.C. and the other acts. L.L. Cool J had a great cameo in *Krush Groove,* which helped break him. But in the end George did eventually fuck us a bit. Unknown to me, he made a deal with the Fat Boys for a follow-up movie, which is how the Fat Boys became so prominent in the movie's final cut. It was in George's interest to blow them up. George Jackson and his partner Doug McHenry hustled their way into making *Krush Groove* their first movie. And they hustled their way to the top of whatever profit was split. They had spent the front part of their lives working on trying to be Hollywood film producers. I had spent mine on records. So it was easier for them, being more sophisticated in film, to take advantage of me. But ultimately I don't fault them; I applaud and respect them. The fact is, for any young black male to get a movie made at that time was a major feat.

There was so much in *Krush Groove* that came from our life at the time. Rick was a student at NYU and we did start Def Jam out of his dorm room, as the movie depicted. The Disco Fever nightclub in the South Bronx and its owner, Sal, were real. The set that was built really looks like the Fever—I get high just looking at the scenes there. For a $2 million budget it was good. But in the end Rick and I were frustrated that *Krush Groove* wasn't as edgy as we wanted. There were a lot of scenes that embarrassed us. They were too bubble-gum.

So we decided to make our own movie. Rick had made one video, but he had attended NYU's film school and wanted to be a filmmaker. So he convinced me and Run-D.M.C. to support him in making a film that more accurately reflected our aesthetic. Jam Master Jay, D.M.C., Joey, Rick and I split the cost five ways to make *Tougher Than Leather,* a film about Run-D.M.C. being harassed by some gangsta types; it also featured the Beasties, Slick Rick, Rick and myself. It started out costing $300,000 but it ended up at $700,000. Eventually we got it all back when we sold it to New Line, though we were never paid a dime in royalties.

We made a silly movie for no money, and if we hadn't promoted it so far in advance of its release, it would have been even more successful than it was. We promoted the damn film like it was a major motion picture. But it wasn't all our fault. It was 1987, right after *Raising Hell,* a hugely successful album for Run-D.M.C. Run-D.M.C. was huge, which made the fact we were making a movie even bigger. So we got all this press—the front page in the *L.A. Times* Calendar section, the front page of the *New York Times* entertainment section, covers of magazines. And it was nothing but a $700,000 movie that really should have been made for

$300,000. And, of course, we didn't know what we were doing. So it was really like Master P's *I'm 'Bout It,* a straight-to-video flick, but it was promoted and hyped like it was fucking *Titanic.* It opened in fifty theaters, mostly around New York, and there were riots when people tried to get in and there were no seats available anywhere. It had one big weekend. But New Line didn't release it nationally, like they would an urban film now. Still, *Tougher Than Leather* was the beginning of New Line's being the preeminent distributor of urban films.

Krush Groove was a heartwarming fake little Hollywood film, whereas *Tougher Than Leather* was a fake street film. So those were my early Hollywood experiences. Both experiences were so much fun that I never wanted to make a movie again.

MODELS AND GUN MOLLS

Now not only was I a budding "music mogul," but my life had been splashed up on a movie screen. That such a thing could happen was a reflection of the impact this new urban culture was having. The roots of the social mobility I enjoy now go back to this period. I'd gone from dating cute Queens girls to punk rock girls with spiky hair to models within a couple of years.

The first model I ever dated I met on the set of *Krush Groove.* Her name was Shari Headley, and she'd later be the romantic lead in Eddie Murphy's *Coming to America.* Sherri was finer than a motherfucker—a tall, light-skinned girl with hair down to her ass. She was gorgeous but also very straight. No one was straighter than Shari Headley. She didn't like no ghetto niggas. The thing that got me over was that they were making a movie about me.

Her mother hated me. Even though they were making a movie of my life, she still hated me. I wasn't shit. I wasn't Eddie Murphy or anyone like that. Her mother's thinking was, "If she's fine enough, she's supposed to bring home the bacon. So why is she bringing this degenerate home?"

Shari was the first girl I bought a real gift for—an $800 diamond bracelet. And she was like, "Thanks." That was it. No excitement. No affection. It was like it didn't mean shit to her. I guess it didn't. Still, I was in love with her. Or I was in love with her uppity attitude and inaccessibility. At the time she was just obsessed with getting ahead and didn't see much future in a hip-hop manager—movie or no movie.

The irony is that through Shari I met a straight-up ghetto Queens girl I actually had much more fun with. This fly girl specialized in dating big-time drug dealers, but she was kind enough to put me in her rotation. I was supposed to put Shari in a video, but then she acted like she was too big to do it. The fly girl, who Shari had brought to my house a few times, really wanted to do it. Her audition was kind of memorable. She came to my house wearing a white fur coat. She came in, laid that coat on the floor and fucked me on the coat. After that Shari didn't haunt me anymore.

Her father owned a bar that was frequented by gangsters, and that girl used to date the most treacherous, murderous niggers in the world. When we went out I'd only take her around the Village because I was afraid to take her uptown, where I was more likely to run into her uptown lovers. I remember going with her to a Luther Vandross concert at Radio City and being scared because there were a lot of gangsters there with their girls. One of them saw me with her, and I had nightmares for days afterward. Despite the danger (or maybe because of it) we dated on and off for a long time.

It was funny that I became known as a ladies' man, but I think it was because I was very obsessive about women. I rarely took no for an answer, and I believe my desire for these women, my never giving up, wore a lot of them down. Despite Shari not feeling my bracelet, I learned the value of gifts. I became known for sending girls bouquets of balloons, and I'd do it every day for a week or more. The idea is simple: I'm not buying your affection, but I want you to think about me because I'm obviously thinking about you.

It also helped that I had an individual style. Back in the '80s I had a uniform—a blue fishing cap, Adidas warm-ups and unlaced Adidas shoes. To be single, black and deep into hip-hop was good for attracting women as the culture developed. And the fact that I wasn't a conformist trying to fit in—that I was making people accept me on my terms—worked for me. Of course, it didn't hurt that I was making money—not as much as I should have, but doing all right.

Eventually, I really got into models because (1) they were tall and fine as fuck and (2) they had an incredible lifestyle. They traveled and were more worldly than the average young woman. Moreover, their schedules were flexible, so I could say, "Come with me to L.A. for the Grammys" and they didn't have to worry about a nine-to-five. They could just pack up the travel bag and go.

From the late '80s right until I got married my girlfriends were models and actresses. As I've said before, style has always been important to me. If you like stylish people, who better to be with than a six-footer with long legs who wears designer clothes for a living?

A funny thing eventually happened. I met one who was the finest, smartest, most worldly, most sophisticated and sweetest woman in the world. Of course, that didn't happen immediately— it took some research to find her.

8 NEW DEALS

From the night that I heard Eddie Cheeba at Charles' Gallery until the late '80s, with Def Jam a hot label and my management company large and growing, hip-hop had made my life better. I dated beautiful women, went to (and threw) great parties and was basically having a great time.

But after that period the smooth part of the ride ended for a while. The late '80s and early '90s would bring changes in every aspect of how Def Jam did business. The first fundamental change was in my relationship with Rick Rubin. From the time we'd met at the downtown nightclub through the building of Def Jam, the two of us had worked in concert. Sure, he didn't like L.L.'s "I Need Love" and a few other moves I made, but essentially we shared the same aesthetic. Then that began to change.

Rick and I were moving in different directions. Rick spent a lot of 1987 working on the brilliant soundtrack for the film *Less Than Zero*. L.L.'s "Going Back to Cali" and P.E.'s "Bring the Noise" are on the album, as were rock cuts produced by Rick, including the Bangles' "Hazy Shade of Winter." While making that record Rick really fell back in love with rock and roll.

During this time he signed Slayer, a loud, supposedly satanic band that allowed Rick to really flex his rock muscles. At the same time I was signing and producing acts in the gritty R&B style I'd liked since the '70s: Oran "Juice" Jones (who had a big hit with "The Rain"), Chuck Stanley ("Day by Day") and Alyson Williams ("Sleep Talk," "Just Call My Name") all reminded me of the groups that I'd loved hearing on WWRL. Slayer and Oran Jones had nothing in common. If we'd been a huge label with many divisions, it would have been fine. But at a small company like Def Jam it was apparent that a real cultural and creative separation was taking place.

In addition, hip-hop was changing in the late '80s. The kind of rap with R&B flavor that Kurtis Blow had been doing came back hipper and cooler through the records Andre Harrell was releasing on his Uptown label. L.L. also played a part in that, which alienated Rick from the music. I don't think he got excited about hip-hop again until N.W.A came out. The New Jack Swing movement that Uptown records and producer Teddy Riley led changed the direction of black music, and Def Jam competed poorly. It would be several years before we got back on top.

Rick began to spend increasing amounts of time in L.A., where the rock-and-roll culture of long-haired bands and loud guitars was still very cool. After "Walk This Way" and *Less Than Zero* Rick was a real hero out there. So while still having equity in Def Jam, Rick moved to the West Coast, started Def American records and became one of the top rock producers of the '90s. His work with the Red Hot Chili Peppers speaks for itself.

The parting was difficult for Def Jam, since many of the acts and personnel had been signed by Rick. Some acts, like the comic Andrew Dice Clay, Slayer and the Black Crowes, went with him over to Def American. So in the wake of his leaving, the corporate culture of Def Jam experienced a profound change. Over time Lyor would eventually become a force at the label, moving from Rush to Def Jam, but that didn't happen overnight.

During the period when I was assuming full control of Def Jam, we were engaged in a battle to redefine our relationship with Sony. We'd made Def Jam the most important real brand in hip-hop. Our roster of L.L. Cool J, the Beastie Boys, Slick Rick and Public Enemy was the best in the game. But below the surface there were some fundamental problems with our Sony deal, problems that got worse with time.

The original deal Rick and I made in 1986 was great commercially—we sold a ton of vinyl and made stars—and bad financially. We basically had a production deal with Sony for Def Jam and not a more lucrative label deal. Under a production deal we got a piece of the profits from the distributor and we paid the artists out of that. As a label, we would have a higher royalty rate and more funding for staff to promote and market the records ourselves. What Rick and I had done was act as if the production deal was a label deal, and we'd been very aggressive in getting involved with every aspect of each Def Jam release. Unlike most people who made these deals, Rick and I still had an entrepreneurial mind-set. We couldn't just make the records and walk away like producers, because we wanted to develop our artists properly. We wanted to leverage Sony's marketing infrastructure, manage our artists through that system and be part of the process. Even if we duplicated some of Sony's efforts in promotion and marketing, at least we could give Sony the proper direction in a culture the industry mainstream was beginning to respect but still didn't understand.

So we ended up hiring employees out of the little bit of royalty points we had from the Def Jam production deal. With that kind of deal the only way to stay in business is to have all hits and no flops, because one flop will wipe out the money from all your hits. After the success of L.L., P.E., Slick Rick and the Beasties, Sony rewarded us by making Def Jam a joint venture with Sony in 1988. In exchange for a 50 percent share in Def Jam, Sony gave us bigger advances, higher royalty rates and more money to expand and pay our staff.

If Rick and I had stayed independent back in 1984, I could have made a lot more money per record sold. But without the power of CBS's distribution and marketing clout, L.L. Cool J, the Beastie Boys and Public Enemy never would have gotten as big as they did. We did that deal for the artists and to grow the culture, but as an owner, I really did not get paid. Def Jam grossed millions for Sony, but I netted only a fraction of the profit generated.

In the record business, companies that have deals like Def Jam's with Sony always go out of business. It's not like the major corporations build all these independent companies and they all survive. It's the profit-sharing structure that kills them. Now, our joint venture was, on paper, a 50-50 deal with Sony. But in reality the numbers were slanted their way. It was only 50-50 after they took 30 percent off the top. Sony had a marketing fee, because I didn't have a full marketing staff. Sony had an administration fee. Sony had a distribution fee. Sony allocated some of their overhead onto our books. Sony had manufacturing fees. Sony charged us more for the CDs than they actually cost to make. The list just goes on and on. Def Jam could gross $50 million but on the books Sony made $6 million and Def Jam ended up $5 million in the hole. The distribution fee they charged on that $50 million was 11 percent. That's $5.5 million right there.

I felt the only way to protect our artists in that situation was to aggressively invest in artist development. We hired people who understood how to market them, knew how to promote them, and could protect them from the big company, which would often make stupid suggestions out of their ignorance of the hip-hop market. That was all good. We built careers for acts that have lasted into the twenty-first century.

Then I made a mistake. I was trying to figure out how to create new profits to share with Lyor instead of sharing what we already had. So I created RAL (Rush Associated Labels), a venture that started a bunch of labels under Def Jam. We attempted to replicate the Sony structure with us being the mother label to several smaller ones, but all of them were unsuccessful. We developed a bunch of product that never came out, because we had no real infrastructure to market them. So I don't even know if those records were all bad. I don't think they were bad—although I think some were not so great. But it was very difficult to put out those records and assist them with the limited resources we had.

So we got deep in debt. Instead of being a new source of revenue, the labels were a drain. Eventually we folded them and I made Lyor my partner in Def Jam, which I should have done in the first place.

One fiscal year the books said we were $17 million in the hole to Sony. Even though that $17 million was fictitious—we were really at break-even if you took away Sony's charges—it put Def Jam in a bad position. So I got into fights with Sony over the numbers. They were also trying to reach around us by having conversations directly with Def Jam artists about signing them to Sony. I mean, really foul shit was going on, like Sony executives were talking directly to L.L. Cool J and to Public Enemy about leaving Def Jam and signing directly with Sony. Sony was preparing to rape me of my company, which is what happens to almost every independent record company.

It's hard under a joint venture to make any profit when you gotta give away so many royalty points when the artists get popular. If you don't share the wealth, then you end up being accused of the same charges of exploitation leveled at Sugar Hill. Yet because we were a small entity distributed by a major corporation, we were really never able to pay P.E. or L.L. in a competitive way. We paid them more than an indie like Profile would pay Run-D.M.C. but less than if they were signed to Sony directly. It got so bad that around 1994 Sony was talking about buying me out or throwing me out. I was feeling mad pressure. One of my side ventures helped me out. I'll talk about *Def Comedy Jam* in more detail later, but it's important to say that its presence on HBO was a big asset during this rocky time. The show meant we weren't just another label. We were a brand in the urban community that was now bigger than just records.

The developer Donald Trump told me that though he was once nearly out of business, his name kept him going. He had enough clout in the larger community that the bank couldn't close him out. This affected all his negotiations in a positive way. I feel *Def Comedy* helped us in the same way by making the Def Jam brand seem larger than just that of a record company. It made Def Jam seem part of the larger culture.

Our brand value is what led PolyGram, a multinational media company who really wanted to be in the hip-hop game, to reach out to us. They figured if you wanted rap, who better to work with than Def Jam? PolyGram struck a deal for 50-50 equity in Def Jam that paid us about $35 million. We got the gross and out of that we paid Sony the $17 million they claimed we owed them. So instead of us being $17 million in the hole, we ended up $15 million in the black after lawyers' and accountants' fees.

The trick of the deal for us was to not let PolyGram know how badly we needed the money. We told them (and they believed) they were bidding against Sony and others for Def Jam. I don't think PolyGram's management ever realized that there was no one else to buy Def Jam. How did we keep this information from them? How come Alain Levy, the CEO of PolyGram, didn't know anything? This may sound strange to you, but he wasn't really connected in the industry. He was a Frenchman who ran an international company, but his links to the inner workings of the business were neither deep nor strong. So he had no one to call to find out how much trouble we were actually in. All he knew was that we had hit acts, our name recognition was high and our contract with a competitor was ending. (We'll get back to Levy and his weaknesses as a businessman later.)

The funny thing is that during the PolyGram negotiations I knew Def Jam was getting ready to put out a lot of hit records. We had the Warren G single ("Regulate") on Death Row's soundtrack to *Above the Rim,* which was the number one single in the country. We were sitting on a Warren G album, an L.L. album, a P.E. album. So Sony started to feel the heat of the records coming out, and at the last minute they tried to jerk us. Sony told us, "We aren't giving you your catalogue." I said, "If you're selling me the company, you're selling me the catalogue." Then we had a fight over the master rights to the Beastie Boys' *Licensed to Ill,* which they tried to hold on to, but eventually they let it go. Lucky for us—it is the most popular album in our catalogue, and one of the most important catalogue albums in the record business. On a yearly basis it sells six hundred thousand units, and when the Beasties put out a new album it does even better.

So finally in 1995 I moved Def Jam over to PolyGram. By most industry standards we should have been over. Instead Def Jam had a new beginning.

This historic move would also begin the next phase of my life. This new period would be defined not just by hip-hop as music, but by its growth as a culture that embraces film, fashion, magazines, television, comedy and politics.

My life in the '90s and beyond moved in parallel with the evolution of all my businesses. Instead of going into my Def Jam office, I got into using faxes and cell phones to move from one enterprise to another. I'd spend hours in a corner booth in the Time Cafe next to my apartment building, making calls and having meetings. Way before it was commonplace, my cell phone was my desk. Maybe because of my training in the streets, I've always been able to keep numbers in my head—royalty rates, radio ads, record sales and, in the '90s, clothing inventory reports, TV ratings and models' telephone numbers. On my new path I've encountered (and often battled) censors, big-time movie moguls, greedy record executives and more models than a Ford agency booker. I also, and this is crucial, found sobriety and my spiritual core. My values and lifestyle have evolved, and I believe all of my business success ties in directly to my internal growth.

PART 2

9 WHITE PEOPLE

During the mid-'90s people started telling me that my company, Rush Communications, was the most powerful, if not the most profitable, black-owned entertainment company in the world. I made the cover of *Black Enterprise* magazine sitting in a hoodie, jeans and sneakers on the hood of a Rolls-Royce—the first businessman in that conservative African-American magazine to rock it like that. It was a sign that the gatekeepers of black culture were beginning to treat me with respect—finally. As defined by many whites and blacks, I'd "made it."

Well, that thought turns my stomach, because in comparison to my white counterparts, my company isn't even significant—at least financially. I'm not saying that to make myself seem smaller. I know my role in influencing pop culture is bigger than that of most of the people I compete with.

From the early '90s till now, my enterprises have been about pushing outside the box of "black business" and growing into the mainstream alongside hip-hop. Most of that growth has been phenomenal—Def Jam grossing $200 million in 1999, Phat Farm licensing agreements worth $150 million, the opening of the dRush advertising agency in 1999, and the launch of my Internet company, 360 Hip Hop, in 2000. There have been some disappointments—Hollywood has yet to be good to me as a businessman, though my time in the city of Los Angeles has been crucial to my growth as a man. In the '80s I spent most of my time promoting hip-hop as music; in the '90s I used that success to expand the reach of hip-hop culture.

Still, to accept the "powerful black company" designation would be to accept living in a box. I'm not gonna do that. In selling to the black community, there's a certain twist you can put in your advertising and marketing to remind buyers it's for black people. But you also don't wanna limit your buyers to one race. The only thing a black businessman might sell that's only for black consumers is hair products. If you are selling Afro Sheen or hair straighteners, your market is defined for you.

But what if you're selling a purple suit? Black people may be the chief buyers of purple suits. You may sell most of your purple suits to black men in the South or Midwest. That doesn't mean, however, that you limit your sales of purple suits to black people. There may be a whole community of white buyers who'd love a purple suit, and you should go get that money, too.

Often black consumers don't like it when you limit your sales efforts to just them because it can feel patronizing. FUBU, for example, has been very effective in communicating with black buyers but not alienating other ethnic groups. FUBU means "for us by us," which is a code phrase for saying it's a black-owned business, which appeals to racial pride among blacks. That, however, does not preclude any hip Asian or Hispanic kid from buying their clothes. With the interest and heat on urban culture we've seen in the last few years, I'd be crazy not to go for the widest possible audience for what I sell.

THE *R* WORD

One key example of how I view the world is my feeling about the word *racist*. I don't use the word *racist* much. It's not productive. It doesn't help me to say, "Oh, yes, white people are racist. That's why I can't get ahead." You see, I realized a while ago that I have the ability to stomach racist white people and accept the rest of them for what they are.

The supermodel Naomi Campbell and I were talking about race one night, and she told me about how she transcended the "black thing" in a hundred ways and does it all the time. "I could be bitter," she once told me, "but I'm not." She went to a white school where some of the students would say shit that was racist to her. But Naomi also knew other white people at school who weren't racist. Those who were racist could be racist all day, but she'd still deal with them the same as she dealt with everyone else. That's why she doesn't mind living, through her work and celebrity, in a predominantly white world—she's accepted that some white people are the way they are. When a cab doesn't stop for her, she calls a Rolls-Royce to pick her up, which I've done, too.

I don't get as upset as my white liberal friends when a cab

doesn't pick me up or some other minor racist shit happens. My friends have a fit about that kind of thing, but I take it in stride, since it is just one of those everyday slights black people expect. I was on a plane talking with one of my best friends, Bobby Shriver, and a flight attendant said something to me like "shush." Bobby said to the guy, "Wait a minute. You didn't shush him, did you?" I said, "It's all right, Bob. I haven't been insulted. Bobby, he didn't shush you—he shushed me." Bobby said, "He did it because you're black." Bobby got madder and madder.

He was shocked because he wasn't aware that I had to deal with that shit all day. He brought it up two weeks later. I said, "Bobby, I don't give a fuck about it. I don't have time to worry about it." Well, Bobby went and got the flight attendant fired—that's how upset he was.

Many white people are shocked by the racism that goes on. They don't see it. I try to get angry, but my anger makes no difference. There's nothing I can do with that anger. So when I say, "I can stomach racist white people," it's because their small-mindedness doesn't mean shit to me. I just go with my agenda and continue building relationships. Anger can sidetrack you. It takes a lot of energy to be mad all the time. Some people can do that and still get things done. I cannot. I have to be moving forward or I fall into the trap of letting the anger control me.

I deal with white people in many areas of my business—music, film, television, clothing, advertising—if they're interested in what I'm interested in, even if they're racists and don't even know it. When they do the obvious racist shit, I just point it out to them. "Look how stupid you are," I'll say. They don't think they're racist even then. "You know what?" they say. "You're right. I wonder if I would have done that if you weren't black." We have a discussion and we laugh about it and that's it. And at the end of the day we're still friends. I'm not saying I'm right to be this way. I'm saying it works for me. I've lived by this code in business all my life. Although I now spend more and more time pushing for change in this country, it's fueled not by anger at any individuals, but by my personal disappointment at America's slow rate of change.

Now, someone could read this and say, "Well, Russell's a millionaire, so he can afford to turn the other cheek." But as this book makes clear, I wasn't given money. I had to find ways to make it. And that means dealing with all kinds of people to advance my agenda. Finding ways to get along with people is crucial to anything you do. A lot of the young businesspeople I meet have a lot of anger toward everyone—not just white people—and go into every business dealing as if it's a battle. Yes, you always have to protect yourself. At the same time you also need to be open. You have to watch everything, be curious about everyone and be willing to be taught. Not everyone you learn from is gonna be nice. Some of them might even be evil. However, at the end of the day, it's what you learn from these interactions that determines your success or failure.

It's simply easier to be in business with people you spend time with. You can discuss ideas with them freely and you can get work done together. If you're in a creative business, you need to have a good working relationship with the people you work with. Real communication has to go on.

I know a lot of successful black people on Wall Street, people like the investment bankers Ray McGuire and Tracy Maitlan. They speak a different language than I do. Obviously we share a cultural connection as black people. But they also speak the language of bankers. Numbers people speak a whole different language when they talk about business. That always makes me reflect on the comment that black and white people speak different languages. I don't believe that's true. Depending on their areas of expertise—be it banking, babies or baseball—they speak the same language on a number of levels except on certain cultural issues.

My point is that I'm more interested in listening to the guy who owns a television network than the guy who works at the network and happens to be black. The guy who owns the network is talking about places and things that I want to know about. If people you meet, white or black, have access to information you want, then you should be talking to them. Race should not be a consideration when people are telling you things that excite you.

DEF COMEDY

A great example of how I do business is *Def Comedy Jam*, which came out of a partnership between two black men and two white men. One of the black men was Stan Lathan, a father figure, inspiration, and life-long friend who also happens to be one of the most successful and experienced television powers in Hollywood. Stan and I partnered with the powerful management company Brillstein-Grey to produce and package *Def Comedy Jam*. Stan and I found the comedy talent, and Bernie Brillstein and Brad

Grey had the juice with HBO to get it on the air. Together we four formed SLBG to produce the show and comanage the talent we uncovered.

The inspiration for *Def Comedy Jam* was a club on Crenshaw Boulevard in L.A. called the Comedy Act Theater. The late comic Robin Harris used to host performances there and was really already kind of a chitlin' circuit legend. He could snap on anybody with his great country-ghetto wit. But he was never mean. There was a warmth about him. His routine "Bebe's Kids," about taking some South Central kids to Disneyland, is a comedy classic that inspired an animated movie. Everybody who went to the Comedy Act knew he was a star. I was among his many fans and wanted to produce a show for him. Initially Stan Lathan and I were trying to develop a sitcom or a movie for Robin. (Tragically, he died of a heart attack in 1990 after appearing in *House Party I* and *Do the Right Thing*.) But after spending time at the Comedy Act, I wanted to work with all the incredible comedians I'd seen there. At the same time the Comedy Act was hot in L.A., back in Harlem there was a spot called the Uptown Comedy Club, which had a similar scene of underexposed black comedians attracting a young, hip-hop generation audience. A light bulb came on. The commonsense thing to do was to expose this to everyone. It wasn't only the fact that the Comedy Act Theater was hot or that the Uptown Comedy Club in New York was hot. Black comedy was developing everywhere. It was happening in L.A., happening in New York, happening in Washington, happening in Baltimore. At a lot of clubs around the country the Wednesday or Thursday night comedy promotion, usually dead nights in the club business, had become their number one moneymaking event. Clearly, by the late '80s the chitlin' circuit in comedy had become a popular young thing, but on the underground tip. So Stan and I, along with Brillstein-Grey, pitched a show to HBO and got a contract to do four shows with sixteen comedians.

I remember going to Eddie Murphy's house with Andre Harrell for a party and having a conversation about who could host the show. At the time Andre was avidly supporting Martin Lawrence for the job. At the party, Eddie Murphy agreed that Martin would be a great host. I don't know if Eddie would even remember, but his enthusiasm on Martin was the thing that put Martin over the top.

So Martin went onstage at the first taping and immediately owned the place. Just from watching his opening monologue, my partners and I knew he was a star. We were lucky enough to keep getting him to host and getting HBO to finance the rising price to do more shows. Look at the talent we had the first couple of seasons—Joe Torry, Bernie Mac, Bill Bellamy, D. L. Hughley, Steve Harvey, Jamie Foxx and Chris Tucker. We broke a wave of comic talents who, to this day, are still the dominant names in black comedy.

What happened with *Def Comedy Jam* was that the top comedians working the circuit got even better because they saw the show as a vehicle that could make them stars. An appearance on the show guaranteed them more national bookings. Then we inaugurated the *Def Comedy Jam* tour in 1993, which promoted the idea among young people that being a comedian could be cool and lucrative. And the black comedy club scene got even hotter. It wasn't just that *Def Comedy Jam* took a scene that was always there and put it on-screen. Yes, there was a strong underground scene before our show, but black comedy really took off and became a huge part of pop culture because of being on HBO.

You know, the show got criticized and accused of a lot of shit by journalists and some blacks, who claimed it promoted negative images of black people. I never ever promoted foul language or told comedians to make their jokes dirty. The most difficult thing about the experience of producing the show was that people thought I promoted nastiness. The truth is, the comedians used their own real language. That's how they talk. Those were their jokes. It was their opportunity to do their routines, tell their jokes, and use their language just as they did in a club, except now they were on camera.

But there were also a bunch of really religious comedians on *Def Comedy* who would never curse in a million years. There were guys on there who talked about the Lord. Some of the comics were even reverends. We presented very diverse subject matter. There was a lot of social and political comedy on that show that gave people insight into important issues. White people didn't all turn on the TV and say, "See how stupid them niggers are." Okay, they might have watched one comedian and said that, but then the next comedian would come out cursing whitey for everything he did wrong. Yeah, some comics were less intelligent than others—and some comics were more intelligent than everyone. There was a little bit of everything on *Def Comedy Jam,* which is why it was so successful.

One of the benefits of *Def Comedy* was that if you were white and watched it, you would discover just how angry black people are. Through the comedy our white viewers found that we're mad mostly 'cause white people are too stupid to know that black people are as good as they are. That's what we get really mad about. Black people don't think they're better than white people—we just can't believe white people don't know we're just as good.

Sidney Poitier and Bill Cosby were both offended by the show's language, because black people in general are conservative about things like that. Bill Cosby is a man who cares about black people, and Sidney Poitier is, too. So I don't have the same anger I used to have toward them for attacking hip-hop or *Def Comedy Jam.* They're just conservative people. When you're a Cosby or Poitier you think it's a good idea to make everybody believe we're all doctors and lawyers. The thinking is if we portray black people that way, maybe the cab will pick us up on the street, maybe they'll make the school system better, maybe they won't redline our neighborhoods.

The problem with that philosophy is that it's wishful thinking. You also need to have a "Fuck Tha Police" by N.W.A out there to force people to confront the consequences of a racist society. You need music and comedy that talks about drugs, messed-up schools, police brutality and all the other community issues that aren't addressed enough in the mainstream—and when they are addressed, it's certainly not from the point of view of the people who are victimized by the conditions. *Def Comedy* was so raw, so honest, so uncensored, it made people who worried about "positive" black images very uncomfortable. Which meant the show did its job.

Def Comedy Jam had a seven-year run. When we left the air we were still the biggest weekly show on HBO. We had an 8.9 rating and an 18 share. Just stupid numbers. It was probably the show that added the most subscribers to HBO of any show in its history until *The Sopranos*. But once those subscribers were in, HBO didn't need to appeal to them anymore.

By the end of the show's run, we didn't have a cool audience anymore. Originally we had a cool audience, but they got bored. What I mean is that the ratings for *Def Comedy Jam* stayed at a high level but the viewership had changed radically. I remember going out to clubs the last few years of the show's run and everybody corny was excited about *Def Comedy Jam* and nobody cool gave a fuck. Everybody corny was like, "That's the funniest show in the world!" Everybody cool was like, "Yeah, I don't go home Friday night to watch it anymore." It seemed like the ratings should have gone down to zero, because no one cool gave a fuck— I certainly didn't watch it anymore. Yet the ratings remained steady 'cause it had crossed over to less sophisticated viewers. By the end there were a lot more white people watching *Def Comedy Jam* than black viewers.

It may surprise some people, but I don't think *Def Comedy Jam* had much to do with hip-hop except that, like hip-hop, it tells the naked truth about our condition. Sure, there were some hip-hop comedians on our show. Chris Tucker, Martin Lawrence and Chris Rock came out of the hip-hop generation and brought some of that edge to their work. But after that the rest of them were older black men. Robin Harris wasn't hip-hop, but he had a hip-hop audience because comedy was a trend among hip-hop heads during his rise. In the beginning *Def Comedy* was a young, cool thing that had an audience just like the one that bought L.L. or Slick Rick. To that extent *Def Comedy Jam* was tied into hip-hop. But it goes in cycles. That same hip-hop audience doesn't really care about comedy now. They still like Chris Tucker. They like Martin Lawrence. They like Chris Rock. But they're not going to see live comedy shows like in the early '90s. Four years into the show's run our audience changed. We had a white crossover audience and a change in the makeup of our black viewers. We went from the hip-hop generation as viewers to older, uncool people with traditional values. It'll surprise our critics, but many of those who came to embrace *Def Comedy Jam* in its last few seasons were church-going, socially conservative people.

Look at the guys on the Kings of Comedy tour in '99. D. L. Hughley, Steve Harvey, Cedric the Entertainer and Bernie Mac sold out arenas all over America. The tour spawned a very lucrative concert film directed by Spike Lee. All four of those comedians received their first national exposure on *Def Comedy Jam*. Yet they all wear purple suits, are extremely traditional in their values and don't have a thing to do with hip-hop. In fact, hip-hop itself became a source of ridicule for many of these comedians and their viewers. These were the same people who every year watched Sinbad's R&B-flavored summer jams on HBO throughout the '90s. So within the young hip-hop audience the comedy trend died. The audience that developed included a lot of older black women who sat at home and watched *Def Comedy Jam* until the very end, who now watch UPN and WB and who supported the Kings of Comedy tour.

At one point *Def Comedy Jam* had two shows touring at once.

Those were big-grossing tours. But they were not as big as the Kings of Comedy tour is in the current market. The black comedy scene has evolved to the point that, as it was with Richard Pryor or Eddie Murphy, it's about artists more than it's about the brand. Slapping *Def Comedy* on a poster no longer has that same impact.

Still, I'm proud to say that despite all the bricks people threw at me and *Def Comedy Jam,* almost the entire landscape of American comedy—not just black comedy—is still influenced by our old weekly cable show. Just take a look at *Rush Hour, Big Momma's House* and *Any Given Sunday*—three of the biggest movies of the last few years, all top-lined by people we helped make stars.

10 HOLLYWOOD 102

For some years after my rough experiences with *Krush Groove* and *Tougher Than Leather*, I'd worked on building Def Jam and only made some small forays back into filmmaking. But a Christmas 1989 vacation trip to Maui got me back into Hollywood. I was hanging with a group of entertainment industry people, including the entertainment manager Jeff Wald, whose son Jordan did A&R for me, and Jon Peters, who was riding high since he'd coproduced the hit *Batman* that year. Peters and his partner, Peter Guber, had taken over Sony Pictures after the Japanese company had paid hundreds of millions of dollars to get him to come work for them.

Peters, with his long black hair, neurotic energy and intense manner, had game for days. On this trip he spent a lot of time telling me how wonderful filmmaking was and how much fun I would have if I gave up the music business. He told me, "Records are for bums." To be a real baller, he claimed, you had to make movies. So he offered me a development deal at Sony. Stan

Lathan, with whom I'd produced *Def Comedy Jam,* had been strategizing with me about developing films and television properties. After looking at our options, we decided we didn't want an exclusive overall film deal with Sony, despite Peters's interest. All we wanted to do was make a film. Somebody at Sony had slipped Stan a script, and Stan slipped it to me. That script was by a young black man named John Singleton. It was titled *Boyz N the Hood.*

I thought it was a powerful piece that had lots of heart and understanding of ghetto life. Unlike the more artsy stuff that Spike Lee had been doing, I felt that John's script had a gritty, realistic quality that could connect with a wide audience. Because of his youth, John had a real love of hip-hop, and it was reflected in his story.

Sony owned the script, but the higher-ups at the company hadn't paid much attention to it. I'll never forget the night I gave the script to Jon Peters. There was Jon, Sony production executive Stacy Snider, a couple of other executives—all female—and a group of other beautiful women just hanging out at his home. He said the most sexist, backward, crazy shit for thirty minutes. Even though he was dating the supermodel Vendela, he told us stories about all these women he had and how he was running them in and out of his house. This was a man who'd started his career as a hairdresser and had bedded movie stars, models, the works. So of course I listened respectfully.

When he finished telling us all that, I gave him the script for *Boyz.* He took the script and told everybody at Sony to make it the weekend read. That next Monday he called and said, "Yes, we're gonna make the movie." It ended up being assigned to

Sony's Columbia Pictures division and its president, Frank Price, who had to be the stiffest white man I've ever met. When I met with Price he asked, "How do we make this movie?" I guess he wanted to hear my approach to production, considering this would have been my first time working as a full-fledged producer with a major studio, and that the director hadn't shot anything but a couple of videos. My idea was to take John Singleton back to New York and let him practice by making some videos, then come back in the summer and make the movie for $3 million.

So while John Singleton was in New York to make videos, Price went behind my back and made a deal with him. John was sitting on my couch in my rooftop patio on the phone to his agent while I was on the Stairmaster. I asked, "John, what are you talking about?" He said, "Oh, nothing." The next thing I knew, Price had made the deal without me. Despite bringing the material to the studio's attention, I was no longer a producer on *Boyz N the Hood*. I never got mad at John Singleton, because he was a young man just out of film school trying to make a movie and I understood his hunger—though I don't think I would have done that.

The only person I was really mad at was Frank Price. That was some scumbag shit he did. When I spoke to Jon Peters, he said, "I can't do a thing, Russell. The guy's got all the autonomy in the world." They actually fucked me. But truthfully, it wouldn't have changed my life if I had produced *Boyz N the Hood*, 'cause they wouldn't have paid me. I would have got a $150,000 fee and that would have been it. I never would have made any royalties.

Actually, in the long run, it ended up working to my advantage. I probably ended up getting $5 million out of Sony because of that movie. Every time I got in a fight with Sony over Def Jam I'd say, "Look at how you treated me on that film." If Def Jam hadn't been with Sony, they would have just screwed me and never paid me. But since I was always negotiating new situations for Def Jam, I'd bring it up as a good example of what bad partners they were. And it was the truth. So until we finally left Sony, their corporate guilt over *Boyz* was a useful bargaining chip for me.

"SUCKING NOBODY'S DICK"

Back in the late '80s I brought Will Smith to Hollywood when he was still the Fresh Prince. At the time I was managing his recording career along with his close friend James "JL" Lassiter. Through Jeff Wald I developed a film script for Will over at Sony. We also wanted to do a television series with him. But Jon Peters and his partner at Columbia, Peter Guber, didn't understand Will. So they blew getting in on the ground floor with one of the biggest movie stars of the '90s.

But I wasn't the only one to see the big-screen potential in Will. I remember I was leaving a West Hollywood hotel to head back to New York when I got a phone call from someone telling me that Will had just left a restaurant with Quincy Jones and an ambitious young Warner Bros. A&R executive named Benny Medina. Benny desperately wanted to be a Hollywood player, and with Quincy's clout and Will's aid, he'd get his wish granted to some degree. Benny pitched Will and JL a concept based loosely on his own life. Then they went to Quincy's house to close the deal for *The Fresh Prince of Bel Air*, while I flew home on the red eye unaware.

The next day I got another phone call: Will Smith wanted to pay me off 'cause he and JL, through Quincy and Benny Medina, had a sitcom deal at NBC. He wrote a check for a quarter of a million dollars to get out of our management deal because he knew we'd spent time and money developing projects for him. I think there was a strong legal basis for us to get the money. However, no one else would have wanted to pay. I respect Will for that. He and JL, who was the day-to-day manager, were very honest and did everything exactly right.

The big lessons of *Boyz N the Hood* and Will Smith are that Hollywood will fuck you if you're only halfway paying attention, which is what I was doing. I was running a record company in New York, going to L.A. to try to make movie deals, then flying back home. I wasn't living in Beverly Hills. I wasn't really a Hollywood person. I was just dabbling in that game, while for everyone I was dealing with, it was their daily hustle.

But I don't regret not being involved with Will's TV and film career, because I wasn't prepared to do a great job with him. I was running Def Jam and spreading the growth of rap music. That was my primary focus at that point. Will really needed a day-to-day manager, which he had in JL and, to a lesser degree, Benny (who no longer manages Will, while JL remains with him). I did not have the temperament to be up under Will 24-7 doing what his managers did. It's hard work sucking up to talent as personal manager. I'm a partner in SLBG Management now, and obviously I used to manage plenty of groups back in the '80s through Rush

Management, which I closed after Lyor got more involved with the running of Def Jam.

But at this point in my life I have no interest in being a doormat. There are no managers who are unapproachable, who can't be cursed out by their clients. So with SLBG they call me and ask me to do certain things for them. But I get worried that some of our acts who blow up big will start expecting me to suck their dicks. That's not happening. A nigga better not yell at me, "Where's my limo?" I don't care if he got twelve movies on line for $20 million a movie. If you call me up and ask me for advice or to make a couple of phone calls that'll help further your career, that's fine. But that's all. You'll need to find somebody else to follow you around. For instance, I'd love to manage Chris Tucker because I know exactly what to do with him. But am I gonna follow Chris Tucker around? No. Am I gonna make him read a script that he's supposed to read? No. I'm not sucking nobody's dick, and ultimately that's what talent management is all about.

THE NUTTY PROFESSOR

With Hollywood back in my blood in the early '90s, I got involved with two of the more eccentric people in the film business, Brian Grazer and Abel Ferrara. Brian is one of the most talented Hollywood guys you'll ever meet; Abel is a true New York underground director. Not surprisingly, the movies I made with each were as different as their personalities and, I think, reflect a lot about me as well.

Around 1992 I started hanging out with Brian Grazer, partner with Ron Howard in Imagine Films, one of the most successful production companies in Hollywood. Brian is a short, spunky, brilliant man with a high-pitched voice and the disarming manner of a surfer dude. Brian would come to New York on business and I'd take him out to go look at models. He was as interested in models as I was. When I first started dating Kimora Lee, who's now my wife, we were sitting at a table with Brian talking about remaking Jerry Lewis's *The Nutty Professor*. My idea was to produce it for Def Pictures, a company Stan Lathan and Preston Holmes ran for me under a deal with PolyGram. I saw it as an $8 million to $10 million vehicle for Martin Lawrence. Brian said, "That's a good idea. I want to make that." So he went and bought the rights to the movie and lived up to his promise by making me coproducer.

Brian did everything he was supposed to do. He tried to get me involved at every level. I guess he really believed that I was supposed to be on the set all the time, chasing people around like a line producer. Or maybe if I was on the set more, he would have been, too. But I was very involved in the whole process of getting the script to a shootable stage. I read all the drafts and gave notes—notes that ended up in the script and that led to a lot of the funny scenes.

But the greatest thing about *Nutty Professor* was the execution of those scenes. The director, Tom Shadyac, who'd done *Ace Ventura: Pet Detective,* was great. He took what was already a great story and shaped it comedically. Then Eddie Murphy brought in the idea that Professor Klump was fat, which was genius and really helped make the movie. In my opinion, the scene at the dinner table where Eddie plays all the Klumps is as good an example of comedic acting as you'll ever see.

So, starting during production and then with more intensity after the film was a hit, Brian started telling people, "Well, Russell didn't do any work. He doesn't deserve any credit." Brian Grazer, as talented as you are—and as much as you can recognize good work—you didn't do shit, either. Nobody did anything but Tom Shadyac and Eddie Murphy and the writers. That's what filmmaking is. It's the creativity and execution of the director and the actors and the writers that make a movie work. The job of a smart, creative producer is to put those people in a room together. That's what happened on *Nutty Professor*. Which is why it always bothered me that Brian doesn't have enough sense to say, "I'm a smart producer 'cause I put all them in a room and they made a great movie." The problem is, he also wants to say, "I was in the room."

I don't know how often Brian's in the room with his other movies, but he certainly wasn't in the room giving directions to those people. He wasn't telling Shadyac how to make *Nutty Professor*. He was just looking at dailies and saying, "That's great!" which is what I did, too.

Brian and I shared producer credit on *Nutty Professor*. After the film's massive success he offered to buy me out of my credit for the sequel. He actually told people that I stole all the credit for the movie, and then didn't invite me to my own premiere. Nor did he invite me to the People's Choice Awards to pick up an award for the film. He told my friend Brett Ratner, the director, he didn't want me there because I'd be walking around the place taking all the credit. When we were talking about the credit for *Nutty*

Professor II, he told me, "I don't want you, with your big publicity machine, taking all the credit from little old me. I do the work." I said, "I did some work, too, Brian. It was my idea." So we worked a deal where Def Jam controlled the sound track for *Nutty Professor II* and Brian would get sole producer credit on that film, while I got my same fee and back-end deal.

I was only paid $600,000 to work on *Nutty Professor* and the same for *Nutty Professor II,* which is nothing by Hollywood standards. I don't know why he was upset. The producer's fee I got was what a nobody gets. Meanwhile he probably made $10 million from *Nutty Professor.* But to tell the truth, Brian would give up all that money just to walk up the red carpet at his own premiere and have the fans yell, "Hey, Brian!" That would be worth $10 million to him.

Brian's a person who comes to a party and brings a picture of himself and puts it on the mantel. He takes it out of his pocket, places it and leaves. I've seen him do it. Brett Ratner had a party recently and he did it. I remember I took a photograph with Brett and Warren Beatty at Brett's house. Later we get the pictures back and there's a framed photo of Brian Grazer in the background. That's just Brian.

But Brian Grazer is also one of the best commercial filmmakers ever (if not the best), which is almost proof that what I've just said about him being a little crazy is true.

ABEL'S ADDICTION

While Brian is a creature of Hollywood, Abel Ferrara comes from another world of filmmaking and art, one influenced by the punk aesthetic that defined the East Village in the early '80s. Now it's no longer as big a cultural influence; it's just another scene. But back then Danceteria, the Mudd Club, Save the Robots, the World—that whole world of clubs, that whole artistic community—didn't care about being commercial, which ironically became their commercial draw.

Save the Robots was one of my all-time favorite places. It was an after-hours spot that I must have gone to for ten years off and on. It was open from five in the morning to two in the afternoon. People there were always throwing up from their drugs, so it had sand sprinkled across the floor. I first went there in '82 with Kurtis Blow, the Clash and some of their handlers. It was like six in the morning, and we were high as hell from sniffing coke. One of the guys in the Clash was throwing up all over his shoes, so a handler went over and gave them some money. The band member took the money, bought some heroin, sniffed it up and then magically stopped throwing up. The handler turns to me to me and says, "Russ, that was the first lesson in management." I didn't really take that lesson seriously, but I understood what he was saying: We were sniffing coke—the good shit—and the band member was sniffing dope, the bad shit. That was my first night at Save the Robots.

Save the Robots was a dark, decadent place where all these crazy "alternative" people hung out. The director Abel Ferrara was one of them. He is a rumpled-looking, stringy-haired man with lots of energy and a total contempt for conventional shit. He's made many movies, but my favorites are *Bad Lieutenant* and *King of New York,* both movies about men driven crazy by a mad mix of religion, drugs and violence that I relate to. I first met Abel at Save the Robots and eventually we became good friends.

One day he came to me with the script for *The Addiction*. It was only sixty pages. He described it to me: "Imagine, if only . . ." And he "imagined" me into financing the movie. The script presented an amazing story, and while I'm not sure that anyone else would agree with me, I'm very proud of that film as an artistic accomplishment.

The Addiction is about a graduate student at NYU who is bitten by a vampire and slowly gives in to her taste for blood. It was shot in stark black and white in the streets of lower Manhattan, a nocturnal world of drugs, obsession and real-life vampires I knew very well. You see, *The Addiction* was about all the shit that I knew. Abel understood the mania of a life where the moment is never good enough, where it's always about the next moment. *The Addiction* is about life as an addiction with blood as metaphor, though the real subject of the film is heroin and how the desire for it can overrun your life.

The script talked about how everything that you think you know about life is worth zero. All someone has to do is tell you that you don't have to live by the rules you were raised on and you could just break them no matter how many books you read.

There's a scene where one character, who's in the process of becoming a vampire, walks through a library saying, "Look at all these books," and meanwhile she's ready to bite a motherfucker. "Look how much we learned," she says. She's just walked from a museum, where she's seen this picture of a guy on a tractor waving at the camera with a grin as he's clearing thousands of bodies off the road. In the photo it's the day after they cleaned the ghetto out. Today's work is to get on the tractor and push dead Jews off the road. No remorse—no nothing. No matter how much education. No matter how much religion. No matter what he's been taught, somebody convinced that man, and almost everybody in his neighborhood and in that country, that it was okay to do that.

So she's looking at that photo and saying, "Why not? Why not do whatever the fuck I want?"

The Addiction will make you shudder and make you scared, and you really never stop thinking about it. You can watch *The Nutty Professor* and forget about it on the way out of the theater. There are some critics and viewers who think *The Addiction* is a great movie—I guess they must be as fucked up as me.

I remember we had a script reading of *The Addiction* at Abel's house one night with two well-known actresses, both of whom were real drunk. I don't know what else they were on. While they were reading they both started crying, "This is so evil! We can't do it!" They'd read two pages of dialogue and start crying profusely. They did this all night.

I'll never forget a screening Abel had of another film. It was at a big Hollywood agency for a bunch of Beverly Hills filmmakers. He was sitting there laughing while the worst shit was happening on-screen. For example, an actress is getting fucked by this guy. Abel yelled, "They're really fucking, in case you don't know. What do you think? That guy is getting the pussy right now. That's fucking real! Not your Hollywood bullshit!"

People couldn't believe it. They couldn't believe he made this thing. At the end they were just quiet. He started clapping. Alone. Clapping real loud.

BLACK OSCAR BOYCOTT

Aside from working with Abel Ferrara, the most controversial moment in my relatively brief film career was when Veronica Webb and I attended the 1996 Academy Awards. Outside the building there was a protest about the lack of representation of blacks in Hollywood. Inside, Quincy Jones was producing the show—the first time a black person had ever done it—and Whoopi Goldberg was hosting. So it was a weird moment: black people protesting outside and two of the most important black people in Hollywood inside playing the most prominent roles in the broadcast.

On the red carpet every other question was, "Well, why are you going? Don't you know that Reverend Jackson's picketing and that black people should be pissed off at the Academy?" To me it's like this: They got to do what they got to do from the outside, and I got to do what I got to do from the inside. When the protesters have left their signs in the street and gone back home, someone has to be there to make the deals, to take advantage of the opportunities that black people have in this society. I wanna be that person. Like the protesters, I don't feel black people should accept the limitations or boxes that white people put us in. But my way of overcoming them is different from theirs.

Specifically, in looking at Hollywood, I feel that a lot of our problems in gaining access to power out there is that blacks in the black film community accept the roles they are assigned. You know you grow up in a racist, segregated world. But if you just accept that fact, if you agree to stay in a self-enclosed black film world, then you are voluntarily isolating yourself. I don't think major producers like Larry Gordon, John Davis, Brian Grazer, Joel Silver or Jerry Bruckheimer are racist. You may meet these people and see some racism in them, but that shouldn't stop you as a black person from doing business with them. If black people didn't do business with white people who have some bit of racism in them, we wouldn't leave our homes every day to go to work. White Hollywood executives you meet are not thinking, "I don't want this nigger to get ahead." They just assume black people don't know anything, because they don't really know any black people. What you're dealing with is not aggressive racism, but cultural ignorance. Brian Grazer doesn't know very many black people. He does know Eddie Murphy, who's not exactly your ordinary black man.

Another part of the problem in the film business is how the few established black power brokers look at the world. Eddie Murphy told me at Brian Grazer's wedding that the reason he doesn't fuck with black filmmakers is that they don't have a big enough vision. I disagree. I think there are plenty of black filmmakers out there with a big enough vision to make an Eddie Murphy movie. Eddie is really Hollywood, which means he is very isolated from the realities of everyday life and is surrounded by people (managers, agents, attorneys) who don't tell him the truth. He's really a recluse, so a lot of what's going on in the world outside his bubble is foreign to him. He's got all the talent in the world, but

RUSSELL SIMMONS

At my fortieth birthday party, friends from all parts of my life stopped by my Beverly Hills home. Here is Andre, Lyor, me, Loud Records' president Steve Rifkin, Stan Lathan, and the late George Jackson.

RUSSELL SIMMONS

A lot of business and bonding is done down in St. Barts over the holidays. On this evening I shared conversation with Sean Combs, Clive Davis, and L.A. Reid.

RUSSELL SIMMONS

Quincy Jones was one of the first established black music people to embrace and attempt to understand what rap was all about. He's been a great inspiration, and I've learned much from him.

RUSSELL SIMMONS

My great life-long friend Spuddy and I. Spuddy was an original member of the Hollis Crew and is still a dear friend.

RUSSELL SIMMONS

This is me with Lauren Hutton, Don Johnson, and my friend Ron Perelman on Ron's boat, Christmas, 1998.

RUSSELL SIMMONS

Donald Trump has been a good friend and mentor to me. This is from a party Kimora and I had out in the Hamptons.

RUSSELL SIMMONS

My wife and I with the honorable Minister Louis Farrakhan. I believe the minister is largely misunderstood, but his work, and that of the Nation of Islam, has been crucial to the lives of hundreds of thousands of people. That's why I'm committed to doing my part to bring him and the Jewish community closer together.

RUSSELL SIMMONS

My father and I chillin' down in St. Barts at my wedding reception. It is one of my great joys to share my success with him.

RUSSELL SIMMONS

Andre Harrell, Allen Grubman, and me on Keith Barish's boat in St. Barts, New Year's Eve, 1996.

RUSSELL SIMMONS

My brothers, Danny and Run, and me. Danny is by far the most creative of us—and also incredibly supportive and generous.

RUSSELL SIMMONS

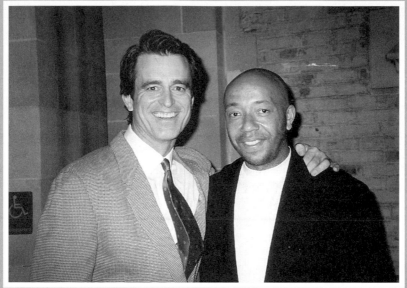

My man Bobby Shriver takes responsibility and credit for my marriage, spirituality, and monetary success. I guess it must be true, since he introduced me to yoga.

RUSSELL SIMMONS

Kenneth "Babyface" Edmonds and his wife, Tracy, have become good friends. He now runs a company with Andre Harrell.

RUSSELL SIMMONS

I backed Hillary Clinton in her successful campaign for the U.S. Senate in 2000. This photo was taken at a fund-raiser I held for her at my apartment.

RUSSELL SIMMONS

I'm so proud of Chris Tucker. He gained a national following on *Def Comedy Jam* and kept on building, to the point where he's now a $20-million-a-movie man.

RUSSELL SIMMONS

Jay-Z and his Roc-A-Fella Records family have been anchors from Def Jam's current golden era. He's a great lyricist whose work should be put in a time capsule so people will understand how many in urban America lived during this time. Here we're courtside at a Knicks' game.

RUSSELL SIMMONS

Kings from Queens: me with L.L. Cool J and Run.

GLEN E. FRIEDMAN

Here I am with my long-time driver and friend, Kenny Lee.

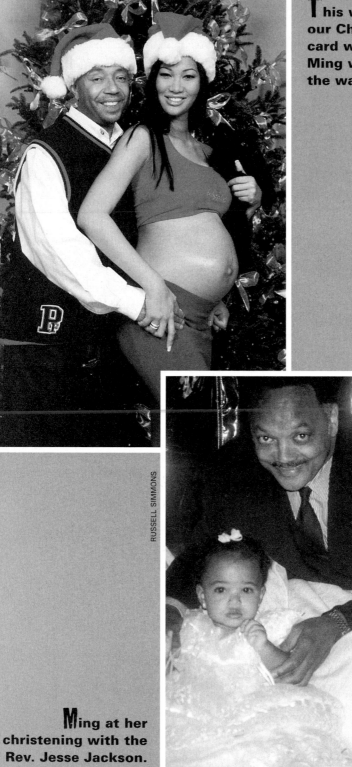

RUSSELL SIMMONS

This was on our Christmas card when Ming was on the way.

RUSSELL SIMMONS

Ming at her christening with the Rev. Jesse Jackson.

RUSSELL SIMMONS

This is one of our first family photos. You can see Ming luckily possesses her mother's beauty.

RUSSELL SIMMONS

My family at the Million Family March in D.C.

RUSSELL SIMMONS

Kimora with Ming Lee's godmother, Tyra Banks.

STEVE ROSS

Steve Ross, my first yoga teacher, who takes life as seriously as he looks. He started out whispering about how many fine girls were in class; next thing I knew, he was pushing scriptures on me.

SHAHAR AZRAN

Here I am at one of the countless benefits I attend, this one with Lorraine Hale of Hale House. The charity has recently been revamped, and I hope it remains viable.

RUSSELL SIMMONS

At the Rush Foundation Annual Holiday Party for kids: me, Danny, Puffy, Wyclef, and Nokio.

GLEN E. FRIEDMAN

Reverend Al getting the gas face.

RUSSELL SIMMONS

At Rush Arts Gallery with kids from the Hudson Guild Program.

RUSSELL SIMMONS

The kids from the CASES Program visit Phat Farm headquarters as part of the Rush Impact Mentorship Initiative.

DEWEY NICKS

One of the first rules of yoga is nonjudgment, even of this photo. Shannon Gannon and David Life run the Jivamukti Yoga Center in New York, a place that's been crucial to my spiritual development.

nobody's talking to him. This isn't uncommon among all huge movie stars, but it's especially true among the biggest black stars.

The fact that the largest black stars live an isolated Hollywood life is important because they are the blacks with the most power in town. The biggest black producers are actors, like Wesley Snipes, who developed his own franchise with *Blade* and produced *Disappearing Acts* for HBO. I find a lot of these actors have the most heart and are smart about relationships and creating images for themselves. When black stars keep their feet on the ground, they open doors and create opportunities, though they can be as ego-driven and arrogant as any white movie star. It comes with the gig.

There are some directors who I think could be great. I think F. Gary Gray, who did *Friday, Set It Off* and *The Negotiator*, is a great commercial director and has the opportunity to be a real player. The Hughes brothers, who made *Menace II Society*, don't work as much as they should, but they have the skills to be huge. *From Hell*, their version of the Jack the Ripper story that they made with Johnny Depp and Heather Graham, is the kind of movie we need to see more of—gifted black filmmakers competing in the film mainstream, yet still interested in making films about black life. That's the kind of versatility we need more of.

But the filmmakers I'm talking about—actors, directors—are talent. There's still no talentless black people riding around in golf carts, the way the white producers do. I'm more critical of the black nonactor so-called producers we have in Beverly Hills. They don't want to compete in the widest arena. They make stories exclusively about black people. They don't understand that black people live in a mainstream world. Sometimes they don't even use white actors. It's the reverse of the black star in the all-white world. These filmmakers act as if black people exist in some world far removed from mainstream society. The production business is about communications, but not enough of the black producers are expanding their base of relationships. I know some will say that white people won't let them in. I don't believe it's that simple. The key to becoming a real player in Hollywood is to first develop a good commercial piece of material that puts black people in mainstream situations—or, for that matter, develop films with white characters. In other words, act like you're in Hollywood trying to make films, not in some isolated wing called black Hollywood. If you're gonna be in the game, be in the game. Otherwise don't act like the studios have some obligation to make your movie. They don't.

BRETT RATNER

I can't end my discussion of my experience in the film industry without mentioning my biggest contribution to the business: my Jewish "son," Brett Ratner, a kid I love like a brother. Today Brett is one of the hottest young directors in town. He made *Money Talks* for no money and established Chris Tucker as a star. He made *Rush Hour*, the biggest-grossing film in the history of New Line Cinema, which took in over $250 million worldwide. With the Nicolas Cage film *The Family Man* he's taken a big step toward being one of the top directors—period—in Hollywood. But when I met him he was just an ambitious kid with tons of energy.

I met Brett through my friend the photographer Glen Friedman, who has been my social and political conscience for the past fifteen years. Brett made a strong impression because he immediately sucked up to me. He'd read in *Right On!* magazine that I wore all these hooded sweatshirts. So the first time Brett met me, he gave me a hooded sweatshirt. The next time he saw me, he brought me a girl. "Russ," he said, "you gotta meet this girl. She's read all about you." In the early days of our relationship Brett was always bringing me something. By day he was attending NYU film school, and by night he was part of the whole downtown social scene of models and clubs. So we started hanging out together. At first our relationship was purely social. I didn't pay much attention to his student films. I remember one was called *Whatever Happened to Mason Reese?* about the child television star. Eventually Chuck D took a liking to him and asked him to shoot a public service announcement for "Rock the Vote." That turned out well, so then Chuck got Brett to shoot a video for "Louder Than a Bomb," which included footage of Public Enemy opening for U2. It was a very well done documentary-style piece.

After that Brett did a bunch of low-budget videos for Def Jam. We'd call him whenever we didn't have any money, and he'd always overperform. He did a video for ex–3rd Bass member Pete Nice for $30,000, which was one of the best videos we'd ever done. From that point Brett continued progressing, doing great videos for Def Jam, Uptown and other labels. His command of the medium kept growing, and eventually he started turning in real slick work like Foxy Brown's "I'll Be."

Part of it was that he hired the best people. Part of it was that he watched every movie looking for shots that he could use. And ultimately, just as he had wooed me, Brett became friends with every artist he worked with, so he was always able to elicit great performances. Even the hardest MC still liked Brett because of his energy and hustle. Chris Tucker's done two movies with Brett and is about to do a third, *Rush Hour II,* which is a testament to Brett's ability to work with people.

Brett refers to me as his "uncle." His mother calls me the father he never had. Whatever you call it, I do very much feel part of raising him. During those early days when Brett was trying to get work, he was always hanging around me. I couldn't turn around and not see him. Our relationship is somewhat similar to that of Sean Combs and Andre Harrell. Andre and I ended up mentoring these guys because we couldn't get away from them. They were hungry for information and wouldn't take no for an answer—and in the end, we loved them like family.

11 CALVIN KLEIN'S A FRIEND OF MINE

There was a time in the early '90s when I contemplated starting a modeling agency, but the numbers didn't pan out. The idea for the agency came out of being around so many models—like every other idea I have for a business, this one arose from my liking something intensely. But seriously, my interest in six-foot, long-legged women had a lot to do with the start of the Phat Farm clothing line in 1992. Models led me to meet buyers and designers and, eventually, into the whole fashion industry.

But before I get into that I want to talk a bit about the connection between fashion and hip-hop. The fashion industry is often right behind the streets in terms of new trends in culture, style and attitude. So in the late '80s a lot of fashion people— designers, models, photographers—started producing their own hip-hop parties. It was kind of an East Village alternative downtown thing, but different from the punk rock crowd at the Mudd Club and the Peppermint Lounge, who'd been the first white audience for hip-hop. Those people were more likely to have been musicians, writers, artists and aggressively anti-mainstream. But there was something else happening in the late '80s—the downtown crowd was no longer just people with earrings in the middle of their forehead.

The club Payday was the real starting point of this transition. It was a dingy but cool little spot in the East Village that had a hip-hop night once a week. It became the place where young models who'd been listening to Run-D.M.C. and seen break dancing in videos could experience the culture, yet still feel safe and comfortable. Payday is where models from the South (like Rebecca Gayhart, now a well-known actress) and the Midwest— the girls who lived in model apartments—began coming out. (Single men take note: Model apartments are where cute little barely-20-year-old girls who just moved into town to build their careers live like five deep.)

When those models started showing up for parties at places like Payday, it began to change the downtown hip-hop scene. The original alternative crowd began mixing with people who were more mainstream in their tastes and came from a more traditional pop place. These young women and men weren't as genuinely rebellious aesthetically as the rest of the downtown kids but were attracted to the rebellion and fun hip-hop represented. Another spot that had this new downtown hip-hop feel was Frankie's Soul Kitchen, where they played old-school funk and rap hits and served fried chicken and 40-ounce bottles of Old English.

In these interactions was the beginning of the mainstreaming of hip-hop culture. An evolution was under way. The white audience was no longer just the edgy East Village people who listened to the Clash and Grandmaster Flash. The audience had evolved to include the people walking through the middle of the Village with designer bags who loved both Madonna and L.L. Cool J.

When Run-D.M.C. rhymed, "No curls, braids, peasy head and still get paid," that meant something—stay rugged. But it didn't mean nearly as much as "Calvin Klein's no friend of mine," which was a clear rejection of mainstream fashion leadership. Hip-hop kids set their own standards of style at that time. That's when the culture was totally alternative. That's when we only wore Adidas and hooded sweatshirts. Dressing up was totally out of the question.

Hip-hop never had dress-up clothes until right about when Tommy Hilfiger started to get real visible, about 1990. His preppy look appealed to the aspirational desires of urban kids, and as that audience began embracing Tommy's clothes, suburban kids started to find them hip. Tommy's designers then began changing some of the patterns and made the logos bigger to cater to the urban market. At this point you saw blacks and whites getting closer in terms of their fashion aesthetics. In clothes, as in music, pop designers started to include hip-hop, and hip-hop aesthetics started to become the mainstream. Most black people have always naturally wanted to go toward the mainstream, to buy into the American dream just the way they saw it on television, just like our white counterparts. The desire can even burn brighter, since that dream is often systematically denied us. So people started to go, "Never mind, Calvin Klein is a friend of mine." Then Grand Puba of Brand Nubian, a New York group influenced by the Five Percent

Nation, rhymed on record about "Tommy Hil" and wearing pink golf sweaters and oxford shirts. Urban sportswear began to evolve from Lee jeans and Adidas sweatsuits into Polo by Ralph Lauren and Tommy jeans.

Around that time a clothing line started by a couple of black people out of Los Angeles, Cross Colours, began to make a mark with loud-colored, watered-down Afrocentric jackets and jeans. One year they were so blazing hot that Cross Colours did $100 million in business. But their audience was extremely young and trend-oriented, so while Cross Colours made a dent, the brand had no staying power and eventually went bankrupt. More important and durable was a designer who'd worked with them, Karl Kani. He came right behind Cross Colours with clothes a little bit more mature—although in my estimation they were still for the young market. Kani's insight was to really emphasize in his designs the baggy, loose fitting style that was already happening in the street. He also brought a distinctive logo to the work, so to this day Kani is still a visible brand in the market. In '92, right behind Karl Kani's success, I opened the Phat Farm store in SoHo. Which, happily, brings me back to models. I used to buy a lot of my model dates dresses at a store on West Broadway called Beguda. When Azzedine Alaïa first came out I remember buying a bunch of $1,000 dresses for all the women I was seeing. Then one day I went to Beguda with a new girlfriend who wanted this red dress that wasn't an Alaïa. I said, "No problem." I put it on the counter and got the price—$3,600! The store's owner, Mark Beguda, was behind the counter and on some old your-girl-can't-afford-this-kind-of-dress shit. So now there was an argument.

I said, "Look, just ring this shit up, man, and stop playing me, motherfucker!" So that day, in a dramatic way, I was introduced to sexy-ass Hervé Léger dresses.

But more important, from that incident I really got to know Mark. Since I was in there all the time buying dresses for girls, eventually we started talking about the fashion business—how it worked at retail, wholesale, marketing—and finally decided to start a company together. We called it Phat Farm. As I talked about earlier, I'd always been into clothes and style as a teen. When I got immersed in hip-hop, I dressed stylishly within the norms of hip-hop—unlaced Adidas shoes, sweat suits, etc. But the parameters of hip-hop were changing in the early '90s, and so was I. Now, I was never going to be a suit-and-tie businessman. I wasn't ever going there. But being around models and fashion opened me up. I ended up learning a lot about designing, retail and fabrics. Phat Farm was the place where I began to manifest this interest in a serious way. My idea was to start with a boutique in SoHo and see how far it could go. We opened the store on Prince Street around the corner from West Broadway. It made sense. SoHo was my hangout. At the time SoHo was also kind of inaccessible to kids, which was good, since Phat Farm wasn't supposed to be a youth-oriented, ghetto-lifestyle company like Cross Colours. It was supposed to be more upscale and aspirational, the kind of clothes I liked and wore.

The early collections were very much an extension of what I wore. For example, I used to wear Sea Island cotton shirts by the British designer John Smedley. So one of the first Phat Farm items was a Sea Island cotton shirt by Smedley with our label on it.

Another early piece was plaid shorts made of Egyptian cotton. We spent a lot of money on our clothes back then. The idea was that the clothes were exclusive but influenced by hip-hop in terms of the loose cut and the use of logos as a design element. The clothes were not modeled after Ralph Lauren's collection but did, in my eyes, have the same classic American style. We made very expensive sportswear, a concept that was unique from a black-owned clothing company. All the others were geared to appeal to the very young. So I saw Phat Farm as the oldest young men's company. That is, it was clothing for someone who grew up in hip-hop, wanted to still dress with that identification, but no longer wanted to wear the same thing a 15-year-old would wear. That was my vision of it.

Yet right away people categorized us as an urban young men's company, because they identified me with hip-hop. In the beginning all the department stores wanted to buy Phat Farm out of the box and treat us like Karl Kani, which meant placement in what was then called the "ethnic" (aka "nigger clothing") department. Now, almost a decade later, that same "ethnic" section is called the "young men's" clothing department, and they have Tommy jeans, Polo Sport and Nautica there alongside more black-oriented brands. Those mainstream brands legitimized our design style and clarified the marketing potential to the department stores and quality retailers, who wouldn't have got it otherwise. And, more than that, the four young black men behind the tremendously influential FUBU clothing line just killed it by exploding as a national brand. This is just another example of how hip-hop, as a culture, faced resistance from the gatekeepers and then was later embraced by the same people who'd resisted it.

To start up Phat Farm in 1992, I put about a half million dollars into it, counting all the production and staff. It took me six years to make a profit at Phat Farm. Over the years I've put $10 million in cash in that company 'cause I believed in my vision. As hip-hop culture grew and the audience grew up with it, I felt Phat Farm would become more and more important. So I stuck with it. But I wouldn't sell to the "ethnic" departments in department stores, because I saw the appeal of our clothes as bigger than that. For that same reason, when I was developing Phat Farm I wouldn't widen my distribution to the obvious ghetto stores like Dr. Jay's, because they wouldn't present my merchandise in a way that supported the brand's more adult image.

But over time Dr. Jay's remodeled their stores and stopped just throwing the clothes around. They now have shop-in-shop concepts for each of the designers, as does Jimmy Jazz, another urban retailer, which allows us to have our own space within the stores. As Phat Farm developed we began to sell to Jimmy Jazz, Up Against the Wall and Dr. Jay's, and also to some of the more exclusive small chains. But our philosophy has always been that we wouldn't sell to just anybody, and we purposely stayed limited in our distribution.

In L.A., the only place you could get Phat Farm for years was in Fred Segal, an expensive boutique on Melrose Avenue in West Hollywood. So let's say you were a kid living in Compton. You had to get on the bus, ride a long way, then get another bus all the way to Melrose Avenue and Crescent Heights to buy a rugby shirt. You'd get there and find out that their T-shirts are $50 and you couldn't afford a rugby 'cause a rugby's $100. So you had to get a T-shirt. Then you had to go all the way back to Compton and hope that T-shirt could get you some pussy, 'cause you couldn't get the rugby. It's too bad that you couldn't get the rugby shirt that day, but you have to respect a brand that does that to you. It was just like when I was a kid and went searching around the whole city for the right sneakers and right pants.

All during the mid-'90s, every time I put $1 million or $2 million into Phat Farm I had a traumatic moment of doubt. I always believed in my vision, but that was still a lot of money to me. One of the worst experiences I had with Phat Farm occurred in 1994, two years after we'd opened our doors. That year we did a licensing deal with a company called USA Classics to service all the retailers with all our goods and then—boom!—they went bankrupt on us. So I had to buy back our licensing rights, which they still owned despite the bankruptcy. I know my friends thought I was stupid and that Phat Farm was a white elephant.

Yet all that time I was learning—about manufacturers in Hong Kong (and India and Korea and El Salvador), about the different urban retail stores, about how to get space in Macy's, about how to talk with the garmentos who dominate Seventh Avenue. Some people might have thought Phat Farm was just a hobby to me, but—just as when I started Rush Management and then made Def Jam's deal—I put the time in and paid attention.

LONG-TERM MONEY

It wasn't until 1996, when Phat Farm was really struggling, that I took my commitment to the brand to an even higher level. That year I went to work running the company myself. And while I was at work, I started exploring licensing again for the first time since the USA Classics fiasco. Licensing means you have a little less control of the product. The licensees pay you for the rights to make products with your logo and brand name. Still, I can tell the licensees what to do, I oversee their designs, and I oversee their marketing.

There are two attitudes to dealing with licensing of a fashion brand. One is to make fast money, like a Cross Colours; the other is to make money in the long term. The short money is for people who just want to exploit their brand while it's hot, making as much as they can over a two- or three-year period before the market moves on to the next trendy clothing style. The long-term money is there for people who own the brand and want to make money in years five, ten and twenty. They do this by building brand value and marketing very carefully. As my history suggests, I'm a believer in the long term. As of this writing Phat Farm has deals for a children's line, bags, leathers, shoes, outerwear, bedding, lingerie, a women's line (Baby Phat), watches, jewelry and fragrances. We've made separate licensing deals with separate companies for all these lines.

For example, we license belts. Those who create the belts for Phat Farm owe me X amount of dollars a year for those rights. I can't lose with them. According to our contract they have to do $1.5 million in belts in year one, $2 million in year two, and $2.5 million in year three. Eleven percent of what they make they have to pay me. If they don't meet their projections, I can fire them—but they still have to pay. Once I fire them, I can move to another company for my belts, at which point the first company's contract is canceled.

What I do all day every day for Phat Farm is manage the licensees and oversee what they do. For example, the shoe guy sits in front of me with fifty pairs of shoes he wants to sell under the Phat Farm brand. I tell him we're selling only one shoe at the present time. He thinks he can change my mind by developing lots of shoes and bringing me the prototypes. But for the time being, I want to stick with one shoe. It's called the Vida—"the lightest, most comfortable athletic shoe in history," according to copy on the shoe's tag. I believe that shoe should sell forever. Not like Tommy Hilfiger shoes or Polo shoes or Calvin Klein shoes, which sell because they have the brand name on them. I want the Vida to sell because it's a classic, special shoe.

Because of my philosophy the shoe guy used to cry every day. Every day. But now he's making a lot of money and can't believe it. He has guarantees to fulfill—he's gotta sell $4 million worth of shoes. So where does he get $4 million in shoes from only one shoe? He's used to shipping a new shoe every twelve weeks for his other licensees. From Phat Farm there is no new shoe. There might be a new color, but it's the same shoe. Eventually our licensees start to get used to how we do business and it starts to settle in. The ad campaign claims it is "the new American classic," and guess what? The Vida did $8 million its first year.

With these licensing deals in place, the company is now fulfilling its potential. I've seen Phat Farm's revenue go from $500,000 to $1 million to $3 million to $6 million to $14 million and now to $65 million. Last year the company did $150 million. This year we are projecting, conservatively, $225 million in wholesale revenue. (When reporting revenue to the press, most companies use the retail number, which is approximately double the wholesale figure or, in this case, $450 million.).

A lot of this growth came from applying what I learned in hip-hop music to fashion: You can't patronize your audience 'cause they're too smart and too sophisticated for that. You can't just jump right into every new trend. You have to have integrity, which is, I think, the most important thing. Integrity is why some artists last while others who follow every trend eventually fall off.

The value of brand integrity manifests itself in clothes in a hundred ways. For example, racing jackets might get hot. But that doesn't mean we'll go make them for Phat Farm. Phat Farm has an image. Phat Farm has a plan. Phat Farm has a well-defined place in the market. So when we create a collection, we create it around a Phat Farm aesthetic, and everything has to fit that aesthetic. If we stretch that aesthetic to capitalize on trends, we still have to be able to give it our Phat Farm touch.

We had an internal argument in 1997 about making racing jackets. I didn't wanna do it, but people around me did. So I allowed my main apparel licensee to make racing jackets. But I designed them. The jackets were called Phat Farm Performance and were decorated with the logos of all my companies: Rush Media, *One World* magazine, Def Jam, *Def Comedy Jam*, SLBG, and *One World Music Beat*. So the jacket's design made it unique to Phat Farm and nongeneric. It was the best I could do to meet the demand and still not sell out my vision of the brand.

Instead of making five thousand dozen, as the licensee wanted,

I allowed them to order a thousand dozen. As soon as the jackets came into the stores, they were gone, and we didn't take any reorders. No store has them left. That's it. The last thing I want to see is a bum dragging that trendy-ass racing jacket around because we put too many out there and it got discounted.

When you find something that's hot and it doesn't fit you, then you have to know to leave it alone. A major sports clothing retailer asked me to make them a million hockey jerseys as an opening order. I'm not doing that. I don't make hockey jerseys for Phat Farm. In fact, for a long time I never sold these guys any clothes. Eventually what we did to accommodate these outlets was create another brand, All City Athletes. I made clothes for them exclusively that were in styles that Phat Farm wouldn't and shouldn't be in. The All City division allows me to get that money that was lying on the table, but still protect the image of my core brand, Phat Farm.

We have a problem now at Phat Farm because we became the leader among urban companies in creating conversational prints. These are shirts with vibrant print patterns. One of our most popular conversational prints has photos of my wife, Kimora, all over it. Absolutely no one else has done as well in the conversational print business. If you go to a party now, you might see two in one place and then two somewhere else. We sold a lot of those shirts. But my point is that conversational prints are a very trendy concept, and I don't want people to think of Phat Farm every time they think of that trend, because conversational prints are gonna be out of style pretty soon. And when that style's gone I don't want consumers to think that those shirts were Phat Farm's main forte.

Right now I'm sitting in a velour suit. It has a crest on it. It's a very, very preppy kind of emblem. It's our version of a velour suit. FUBU has a velour suit with great design and three hundred colors in it. And that's great—that's a great FUBU suit. I have a black velour suit with a crest on it—that's a good Phat Farm velour suit.

I'm stuck on the word *classic*. At my advertising agency, dRush, I like to get accounts that don't need me to be trendy. For instance, there's a client—a beverage company—that we have now who put some of my music acts on the side of their product before I actually ended up doing advertising for them. And the bottles were selling like crazy. The gimmick was getting people to start to pay attention to their product, but their whole campaign couldn't be based around just giving away these music artists. It's good to be associated with these artists, but there are more lasting ways to get to that audience.

In that company's campaign there needed to be something more significant about the lifestyle they were trying to promote and, more than the lifestyle, about how the beverage fit that lifestyle. You try to sell a certain beverage, so you want to talk about that beverage. If having music artists on your bottle is the only campaign you've got, you're damaging your position because you're focusing attention on a gimmick instead of on your product. You've got to create an attitude that the beverage is something lasting and stable and honest, not gimmicky. Gimmicky is always a problem.

If you step over your boundaries, as sometimes you do in the music business, you can look back and say, "You know what? This record is a little more commercial than the guts of the artist." But if the artist does a lot of things and has diverse subject matter, it's fine. The same applies to clothing. If the clothing line is diverse, then it can get away with having some things that are simple, subtle and classic and some things that are more aggressive and trendy.

But if Phat Farm does too many pieces that are aggressive and trendy, I might look at my collection in the store and see stuff that doesn't fundamentally represent what we're trying to sell. If we sell a garment that doesn't represent Phat Farm well, then we have to make a statement in my merchandising and marketing that reaffirms who we are.

I don't want people to form the wrong opinion. Who do I think I am? Classic American style. What's in my ad? A racing jacket? No. An oxford shirt.

THE GLAMOROUS LIFE

In the '90s, as I was developing Phat Farm, moving Def Jam to PolyGram and in general trying to grow all my media businesses, I lived in Greenwich Village and TriBeCa in Manhattan and, for a couple of years, in Beverly Hills and Malibu. Certainly where I lived and who I met in these places influenced me in how I marketed hip-hop culture. The people I encountered and befriended in these upscale environments helped me see how the culture was going mainstream and find links where other people saw barriers.

In 1990 I found that the fashion-forward, trendsetting crowd went to the Hamptons on summer weekends, so that's where I went. The Hamptons are a series of beachfront towns near the eastern tip of Long Island where the financial, fashion and media elites of New York keep summer homes. Actually, the catalyst for that move, as it was for a lot of my moves during that period, was a fine woman. Cynthia Bailey, a smart, gorgeous model I had dated in the late '80s, and another fine friend were going to the Hamptons for a weekend. Sounded like where I should be.

Around this time the transition of hip-hop into the mainstream was really starting to happen, and the Hamptons crowd helped make it happen. You'd go to a Hamptons party and hear rap records, every summer more than the year before.

That jet-setting crowd carries messages all over the world, and the message that began leaking out from the Hamptons was that hip-hop was fun, accessible music. The tastemakers in media and the financial world began feeling this. It slowly began affecting the amount of media attention the culture received, how the fashion industry perceived urban fashion and how Wall Street viewed investing in hip-hop-related businesses. I always believed in advertising to tastemakers. If my budget is limited, I'd rather buy an ad in a magazine the Hamptonites read than in some big mainstream magazine. If I can get the Hamptonites to make a statement by adopting a particular aesthetic, then it grows organically from the cool fashion community to the rest of the crowd. Other people want what they wear, what they listen to and what excites them.

Black people, in particular, are very aspirational, which is why they find Ralph Lauren and similar brands cool. These brands were originally established in places where people are successful, and the brands became associated with success. Since black people crave success—a success historically denied us by racism or poverty—we wear these brands to celebrate whatever success we attain. That's why many trend-setting black people read the luxury consumer magazine *Robb Report*, to stay on top of trends in high-end merchandise. That's why they buy particular brands. They're paying attention to what goes on in terms of fashion, cars and brands in the Hamptons and Beverly Hills. So I say, "Let's get the Hamptons and Beverly Hills to do what we tell them. Then they'll get the rest of the world to follow."

I should also mention that in those places, where everyone's floating around with the most money, flyest cars and most expensive toys, you find the finest girls. The Hamptons are where the tall, skinny girls are every summer, which was definitely a big part of why I was there. And I loved the fact that models were helping to carry the banner for hip-hop culture.

I started going to St. Barthélemy, a beautiful, small Caribbean island near St. Maarten, for Christmas for the same reason I went to the Hamptons. The people there are fashion-forward, elitist, exclusive and trend-setting. I first went in '91. One reason St. Barts is so exclusive is that it's very hard to get there. First you have to fly to St. Maarten, then take a small boat or a tiny little plane to St. Barts. I remember taking the boat because it was too late for the little plane. I got seasick during that short journey, and when we finally got there I lay on the dock feeling horrible. But when I finally got to the party I had come for, I immediately felt better. I couldn't believe it, but I knew almost everyone there. Actors like Uma Thurman and Bobby De Niro. Models like Naomi Campbell, Gail Elliott and Angie Everhart. Producers like Brian Grazer and Cary Woods. The great record men Clive Davis and Seymour Stein. Everywhere were designers, fashion editors, and plain old successful motherfuckers—people who either were or would soon be supporters and collaborators in my various ventures. It's different from seeing these people in a boardroom at the Sony Building or a showroom on Seventh Avenue. Meeting them on a boat in St. Barts and hanging out with them, their spouses and their kids is what builds a strong relationship. Many of the connections I've made in the Hamptons and in St. Barts have been crucial to Phat Farm in particular and to my development as a businessman in general.

12 MEDIA MOVES

One of my favorite hangout buddies and inspirations is the great record producer Quincy Jones. I first met Quincy back in the mid-'80s when I threw a party for his son, QD III (later to become a fine rap producer), in New York with lots of the rappers I managed. Quincy has a warm, embracing presence, and over the years he became a mentor to me. In the '90s, as I started to expand outside music, he gave me lots of good advice. One day I told Quincy I wanted to be involved with *The Source*, which was the biggest and best magazine covering hip-hop. Quincy said he wanted to be involved, too. To be involved with a magazine about the culture I worked in every day seemed like fun.

So we had a meeting with *The Source*'s owner, Dave Mays, and talked to him about making a substantial investment in the magazine and taking a controlling interest. Quincy's Qwest label was distributed by Warner Bros., and he felt Time Warner would back our venture. He was right about their interest, but eventually

Time Warner's involvement became a stumbling block. Time Warner wanted a much bigger interest than Dave was willing to sell. Their offer was way too aggressive. It was almost like a dis to Dave. I'm sure he looks back on it and thinks we were a bunch of assholes trying to take control of his asset.

After Dave rejected us, Quincy got Time Warner to fund the launch of a brand-new magazine, *Vibe,* to compete with *The Source.* So Quincy and I went to work to find an editor in chief who would satisfy Time Warner. We submitted the names of a bunch of different editors, but none was deemed acceptable by Time Warner. Eventually word came down that the suits up there wanted Jonathan Van Meter to edit our magazine. People I talked to in the media business warned me, "If you don't approve him, Time Warner is likely to drop this project."

So Time Warner set up a meeting with Jonathan. He did have publishing experience and knew about managing a magazine. What Jonathan didn't know was the first thing about hip-hop. When I asked him specific questions about the culture, his answers weren't far off, but none suggested any real love of hip-hop. At one point he said, "I know all about dance music and hip-hop," which was like saying "I know all about ballet and break dancing." You know what I mean? Jonathan acted as if dance music and hip-hop culture were the same thing. I told him, "That's the most absurd concept in the world that you can lump those things together. They are opposites, and there's gonna be a problem if that's how you edit the magazine."

I told Jonathan that if he wanted the job, the most important thing he had to do was to surround himself with people who understood and were familiar with the culture. The next thing I knew, he hired a guy who knew hip-hop but who people in the community suspected was gay. In fact, Jonathan was gay, as were several of the editors originally at *Vibe*.

Now, if Jonathan had been editing *Harper's Bazaar*, this sexual orientation wouldn't have been an issue. But hip-hop is absolutely the most homophobic, macho culture that's influenced mainstream America in a lot of years. In painting, dance, fashion and theater the gay perspective is respected and valued. Gay people are generally accepted in all forms of art in America. But homosexuality is a real issue in hip-hop. It's unfortunate, but it's absolutely the truth. So for *Vibe* to start with so many gays making editorial decisions just seemed like a bad idea in terms of how the hip-hop community would view it.

Still, even after Time Warner hired Jonathan, I stayed with the magazine and worked with the *Vibe* staff on concepts and marketing. But right before the launch, a promotional brochure was released to position the magazine. In this brochure it said that Madonna and Sandra Bernhard were part of the fabric of hip-hop culture. I said, "Fuck y'all. I resign!" I respect the work of both those women, but they are absolutely not related to hip-hop. It was that warped perspective—one that equated Madonna with Def Jam as if the two were the same thing—that informed *Vibe* during its early years.

From the day I resigned to right up until yesterday, I've had issues with *Vibe*. I felt they treated my company really badly over the years. It feels like there have been ten stories on Bad Boy and Death Row for every one on Def Jam. New editors would come and go, but the negativity carried over. Finally I've developed a good relationship with the editorial team there, and in the last few years they've been very fair to me.

BRANDING BIZ

The business start-up that's taken up most of my time these last few years has been my Internet company, 360 Hip Hop, which should be the most engaging site about hip-hop on the Internet. It should be a walking, talking, fun, interactive version of the culture online. To start it I got Seagram and Sony engaged and supporting me. I also received investments from Queen Latifah, Will Smith, Jay-Z, Tyra Banks and a lot of other talented people. The concept is to get them involved in the site—not contributing to it creatively or promoting it exclusively, but invested in it in a proprietary way, so when we send them a memo they might actually read it, talk about it and make their opinions about it known. It's a fashion-heavy site where we sell Phat Farm, Sean John, Mecca and Tommy Hilfiger. Some of these brands are exclusive to our site, and others will benefit in big ways from being associated with our site. We're looking to become the best fashion fulfillment house on the Web.

After launching 360 Hip Hop in spring 2000 and operating on our own through the summer, we made a deal with BET in the fall that will allow us to fulfill our strategic goals and cut our overhead. As anyone who reads the newspapers is aware, so many Internet start-ups have spent themselves right out of business. In our deal 360 Hip Hop joins with BET to share technical and marketing efforts, while we maintain control of our content. We serve the hip-hop market, and BET serves the more general African-American audience.

The partnership doesn't just make economic sense, but puts myself and BET's CEO, Robert Johnson, in business. Johnson has used the BET cable network as a base to build a huge media enterprise, which he just sold to Viacom for $2 billion. So for us to be linked through this deal is, I believe, quite historic within the history of black business in this country. We are two black entrepreneurs who've managed to build businesses from scratch, give hundreds of black people jobs in growth industries and maintain strong business ties with Wall Street and corporate America. Those are a unique set of qualifications, which I see us exploiting in tandem well into the twenty-first century. It also serves 360 Hip Hop's political agenda, since BET, our strategic partner, is sensitive to our role as an advocate on issues that affect our community. Some of the best content on 360hiphop.com deals with serious issues affecting young people. We had on our site a graphic that illustrates the forty-one shots the New York City police put in innocent African immigrant Amadou Diallo. As you click on each bullet hole, a video bite of someone talking about police brutality or racial profiling appears on your screen. As an extension of that attitude, 360 Hip Hop sponsored a Rap the Vote campaign to register young people. In August 2000 we supported a march on Washington, D.C., aimed at getting the nation "to redeem the dream" Martin Luther King Jr. spoke about at the original march on Washington in 1963. This rally wasn't about segregation but about the social and economic problems of the new century. Alongside Reverend Al

Sharpton and Martin Luther King III, we drew over a hundred thousand people—primarily young people—to energize them around the issues of police brutality and racial profiling, among other matters. In the long term we're beginning the process of activating the huge potential of the hip-hop generation as a political force, and 360 Hip Hop will be a key tool in making that a reality.

On October 16, 2000, through my companies Phat Farm and 360 Hip Hop, I helped sponsor the Million Family March in Washington, D.C., an event that drew hundreds of thousands of people from all over the country, featured scores of celebrities (including Will Smith and his wife, Jada), was broadcast live on BET and showcased a historic speech by Minister Louis Farrakhan. In that speech, which the Minister allowed me to discuss with him hours before he presented it, he embraced a more humanistic approach to race and religion, and talked about his constituency participating in the presidential election. There is no question in my mind that the efforts made via the website and both marches helped stimulate an increased number of blacks to vote in November 2000. So from a fashion, e-commerce, political and overall content viewpoint, 360 Hip Hop is just another vehicle for the distribution of the ideas and culture of hip-hop.

THE BROKEST NIGGER IN THE ROOM

I've been in the advertising business since 1996, when Rush Communications did our first Coke commercial. We've done about a dozen since. Our first spot, "Father & Son," speaks very well to my philosophy of hip-hop as mainstream culture. The commercial began with a middle-aged black father drinking a Coke and listening to Marvin Gaye and Tammi Terrell's Motown classic "You're All I Need to Get By." Then there's noise from upstairs. We pan up, and his son is blasting Mary J. Blige and Method Man's bangin' update of that record as he sips a Coke. Everything in that spot is classic—both versions of the song, the way we dramatized the generation gap and, of course, Coke. That we used music as the link speaks to our understanding of how it works to both represent and span generations, just like Coke does. "Father & Son" was Coke's number one commercial among young people in '96. Brett Ratner did the spot for us, and I believe it's in a class by itself.

Since then we've created ads for ESPN and a tribute to Ron Brown at the 1996 Democratic National Convention. Our street teams have done groundswell marketing for Coke, HBO, Estée Lauder and Tommy Hilfiger. Mostly we've done creative work. But we weren't big enough to do the actual managing of the entire marketing process until 1999, when we partnered with the Deutsch Agency to create dRush. In the year 2000 we expect to do at least $50 million in business. But that's just a start. Deutsch itself is a $1 billion enterprise. That's the bar I'm looking at.

With dRush I don't see myself in competition with the black ad agencies, because I don't accept that I'm a black ad agency. The fact is that the black advertising business could become an obsolete business—just like black distribution for clothing has become, just like the black record business should be. I hate the idea of "black business" because I'm part of a newer generation. The guys who built black businesses in the past did what they had to do. They were talented, smart people who figured out a way to get paid by servicing their community.

But the African-American community is way too powerful for the people who are smart about business in our community to be limited to making ads only for black people or selling clothes or records only to them. Once our people were happy to get an ethnic clothing department. Once our people were happy to get a black film division, where the major studios hire three niggers to make $5 million movies. Once our people were happy to get black record divisions 'cause that was the only job we could get at the major labels. But we shouldn't be happy about that anymore.

My business is multiethnic. It's one culture, but it's multiethnic. You have to have enough vision to know that you're not breaking any ground because you're the biggest black company. You're breaking ground when you're competing with the real mainstream British, German and Japanese companies. Whatever the gross numbers of my companies combined, it doesn't add up to anything in comparison to a lot of the people I'm around. I'm not looking to be the richest or most powerful person I know—I'm just looking to be able to go somewhere and not always be the brokest nigger in the room.

For example, I'll never forget traveling to a fight in Atlantic City on Donald Trump's plane. Everybody on it was richer than me except the gossip columnist who tagged along. On board were all these guys who make and sell unglamorous things, all worth many more millions than me. Yet when I got off the plane, everybody's waving at me and Donald because we have public images. I have the image of some great black entrepreneur. But I'm with my man Donald Trump, who owns the fucking building the fight is in. The building's so huge, you can go joggin' in the bathrooms.

I go in the building and people are saying, "You the man, Russ," as I walk by. I'm with the guy who has the biggest casinos and residential buildings in the world. There are thousands and thousands of slot machines and poker tables in just one of his many buildings. So that's the magnitude of the real successful mainstream entrepreneurs versus black niche market entrepreneurs. Now, in the twenty-first century, I think there's an opportunity, with black culture being so strong and racism somewhat relieved, that we can own some things and build our businesses beyond servicing niche markets. The energy and creativity of black art and culture has been the engine driving American art and culture for decades; it's time that black businesses use that same energy and creativity to compete on the widest possible playing field.

Trump has been very influential in helping me expand my vision. Sometimes I talk to Donald two or three times a day, and he's taught me many things. The best thing was a story he tells about buying a building. When he built Trump Tower he also bought the rights to use the Tiffany name on the building. It was gonna be Tiffany Tower. His late father said, "Yeah, right. When you change your name to Tiffany, you call it Tiffany Tower. But for now you call it Trump."

Over a period of many years, whenever he was in trouble, his name and his promotion of himself as a brand are what saved him.

I keep that lesson in mind. I remember how connecting *Def Comedy Jam* to Def Jam records helped both entities—associating HBO with an established hip-hop brand helped get the show on the air, while linking the label to a hot TV show helped the label survive a cold period.

13 NIGGAS WITH ATTITUDE

The coldest year in Def Jam's history was probably 1990. We had been the dominant hip-hop label and set the standard for East Coast hip-hop. We still had L.L. and Public Enemy, but as I noted earlier, we were in the middle of our troubles with Sony, so we were vulnerable. Starting with N.W.A's *Straight Outta Compton*, acts from L.A. and elsewhere on the West Coast began filling the vacuum by borrowing the aggressive style and swagger of acts like Run-D.M.C. and Public Enemy.

The West Coast scene at that time was really antimainstream, countercultural, aggressive and young. I always say youth culture is based on the desire for change, and the West Coast started to speak to that better than we did back East. Their view was uncompromising: "I want to change the world. And if I can't change the world, I'll just take what I want from it." As negative as that sounds, it's still not as bad as what alternative rock was saying at the same time, which was "I'm just gonna take drugs and kill myself." Although there seems to be nothing positive about pro-gang records, they do teach listeners something about the lives of the people who create them and remind them that these people exist. At the time gangsta rap became popular, no other medium was giving voice to the struggles of poor urban young people in the age of crack.

A lot of that West Coast creativity was fueled by resentment of the power New York held over hip-hop. The East Coast (primarily New York, New Jersey, Philadelphia and D.C.) had a lot of power in marketing, promoting and breaking acts. Whether it was BET, *MTV Jams* or the editors of rap magazines, all of these key hip-hop media outlets were (and still are) heavily influenced by New York hip-hop DJs, whose playlists reflect local taste. As a result, things happening musically on the West Coast and in the South were not getting great support from New York tastemakers. This made it difficult for these acts and their culture to be exposed in the same way that New York was exposed in Los Angeles. New Yorkers started to take their dominance for granted and became elitist, and that's why L.A. kicked our ass so hard. We in New York were no longer making what America wanted to hear, and L.A. was.

Lyrically, West Coast hip-hop took street narratives on records to another level of violence. At the same time, they took the sound of hip-hop to a higher level of pop acceptability by using strong melodies. That wasn't apparent in *Straight Outta Compton*, N.W.A's breakthrough album, but it became more obvious with time. West Coast producers like Dr. Dre and his brother Warren G made records that had violent lyrics but were melodic throughout. Then, shrewdly, they made beach party videos for the songs, playing into our dreams of the California lifestyle. They'd make violent records, but the videos had girls in thongs, G's in low-rider cars and people playing volleyball. Compared to videos of New Yorkers in hoodies in front of the projects, that West Coast shit looked like fun. Still, what held it all together was Dr. Dre, the most talented producer in rap, an original member of N.W.A, and cofounder of Death Row records. A record like "Nuthin' But a 'G' Thang" off Dre's *The Chronic* album was a huge pop hit, despite its gangsta lyrics, because the feel of the record was big, melodic and beautiful. With records like that, Dre balanced the light and dark sides of L.A. like a damn acrobat.

Def Jam's response to the West Coast was to become a truly national company. We signed the South Central Cartel out of L.A. and made a record with them, *N Gatz We Truss,* that was very violent but full of social and political insight. We had a couple of huge pop hits with another South Central act, Domino. We signed Montell Jordan out of L.A., who's developed into the most successful R&B act Def Jam's ever had. And Lyor Cohen, who by now was running Def Jam's day-to-day operations, really turned things around by personally going out west to sign Warren G, whose "Regulate" became the biggest single in Def Jam history.

That Warren G was also Dr. Dre's little brother meant two things: one, he had a real pedigree in the game, and two, it raised a few eyebrows out in L.A. that Def Jam had him and not Death Row, which Dre's production skills and recordings had made the leading label out there. In a lot of people's minds, signing Warren G put Def Jam in conflict with Suge Knight, the six-foot-four former football player who headed Death Row, the man who helped push West Coast hip-hop to new heights and, before his incarceration for a parole violation in 1998, the most feared figure in the game.

SUGE, TUPAC AND BIGGIE

Suge's reputation preceded him. He wasn't just a big man; he was reputed to be a member of the Bloods, one of L.A.'s largest gangs. He was also known to be quite bold. According to legend and lawsuit, he had gotten Dr. Dre away from Eazy E's Ruthless label, with some I-made-him-an-offer-he-couldn't-refuse shit. I don't know if any of this was true, but it gave Suge one hell of an aura when he walked into a room.

But, in truth, there was a little friction with Death Row when Warren G joined us. I personally never got any real pressure from them. But rumors of a possible beef created some concern on Lyor's behalf, since he was the one traveling out to L.A. to handle Def Jam business, so we hired some security when he went out there. There were no threats against me from Suge, however. There were people out in L.A. talking negatively about me, mumbling shit like, "How dare he sign a West Coast act that should be on Death Row." But Warren was free at the time, and we signed him. Def Jam was doing its job.

Despite the fact that on record and in interviews rappers from both coasts talked bad about each other, I never ever received any hostility from Suge. He was gentle when I spoke to him. His attitude was like, "I'm a big, giant motherfucker. I could crush you with my hand. But I'm not bringing that attitude your way." If I needed a favor from him—a record for a sound track project or an act of his to appear at a promotion—he'd give it to me. If he needed a favor from us, we'd give it to him. People forget that Warren G's "Regulate" was on the *Above the Rim* sound track that was released on Death Row records. Tupac, then signed to Death Row, starred in a movie, *Gridlock'd*, that I helped get made. So we did business together several times without any disputes.

What's the message of all this? I believe that if you create bad energy, it comes back at you. I've never had a major beef with anyone or any group in the rap business. Never. I've never had a bodyguard in my life. Maybe there were times when I should have had one, but it never occurred to me then and I don't wish to start now. In my opinion, negativity breeds negativity.

Tupac, who signed with Death Row in 1994, was always great with me. Despite the gangsta image he cultivated, whenever I would run into him at the Bowery Bar in New York and other glamour spots, he always had love for me. I mean, I never even heard him raise his voice in my presence. Despite his rep for acting reckless, I never saw Tupac act crazy. I know this must sound like I'm in denial, but I'm being very frank. I heard all the negative, scary records he made, like "Hit 'Em Up," on which he threatened Puffy, Biggie and everyone at Bad Boy records. I don't know if the words were just theatrics or if Tupac really felt all that hate in his heart. But people say he was capable of partying one second and then shooting bullet holes in the ceiling the next.

Often in New York I'd see him hanging out with Mickey

Rourke. That was his man. They'd made a direct-to-video movie together, and after that they hung out all the time, acting like bad boys. I remember one night being at a Christy Turlington–hosted function at a New York hotel. It was a little benefit for some disaster in South America and everyone was wearing tuxedos. Then Tupac and Mickey Rourke walk in like they just broke down the doors, like a dramatic scene in *King of New York*. Tupac had on his bandana, a silk suit and sneakers. And fucking Mickey Rourke just looked like Mickey Rourke with his shades and slicked-back hair. I'm sure he eventually found out that when you hung out with Tupac, anything could happen. The truth was, Tupac Shakur was a real bad boy, and Mickey Rourke just plays one in the movies.

Way before Tupac signed with Death Row he had crew all over. He had crew in Baltimore, where he spent much of his childhood. He had crew in San Francisco, where he recorded with Digital Underground. He had thugs to hang out with in every major city. But the niggers he hung with from Queens were rough. How rough? People whom I think killed people, whom I think had bodies, were scared of the crews Tupac rolled with from Queens. So Tupac may not have been a real gangsta, but he knew thug life for real and his records were full of real information, not just fantasy.

I didn't know Biggie Smalls, aka the Notorious B.I.G., as well as I knew Tupac. We'd met through Puffy and Andre Harrell a few times but weren't close, though I just loved his lyrical attitude. Biggie was one of those rare poets able to translate any experience into vivid, cinematic and often funny word pictures. No one made you "see" his rhymes like Biggie. Unfortunately, my most vivid memory of him is from the night he was killed. I was with Biggie just ten minutes before he got shot. I was with him that whole night at the *Vibe* magazine party out in L.A. We sat at a table laughing and drinking. He had a cane because he was recovering from a leg injury. When Tupac's "California Love" came on, I'll never forget how Biggie held up his cane and bobbed it in the air to the beat. He loved that record, despite the fact that Tupac—who at that point had been dead about a year—had attacked him so often in interviews and on record. That night he was happy and all that mess didn't seem to concern him. I never would have thought in a million years he was gonna get moped when he went outside. I never would have thought that.

Compounding my sadness over Biggie's death was that it happened outside a party held by a magazine that threw many logs on the East Coast–West Coast fire. The antagonism that had started in the early '90s between rappers in L.A. and New York had become centered around Death Row and Bad Boy, Suge and Puffy, Tupac and Biggie. In hip-hop it wasn't unnatural, or even unhealthy, for you to have competitors you tried to outdo. It had been that way since DJs, MCs and breakers battled in New York parks. But no one called it the East Coast–West Coast war until *Vibe* named it and, by doing so, inflamed it. Biggie and Tupac could fight all fucking day. Their personal beef had nothing to do with people outside their circle. Labeling it an East Coast–West Coast war on newsstands all over America was the act of irresponsible people who didn't understand the community well enough to know what they should and shouldn't do. They took an internal industry beef and played it in such a way that niggas in the hood were feeling it. *Vibe* helped make it seem like it was an act of regional loyalty to dis people and records from the other coast. This stance may have sold magazines in the short run, but overall this coverage was bad for hip-hop.

A prime example of what I'm talking about is that *Vibe* published a list of all the things that happened in this so-called East Coast–West Coast war. They didn't make it just a list of incidents involving Tupac and Biggie. They took unrelated events, wrapped them between the Tupac-Biggie beefs and created an artificial timeline that suggested an ongoing battle between acts from both coasts. In essence, they took a beef between two men and two labels and made it seem like an African tribal war. Between that list and the covers they ran, *Vibe* was morally and journalistically wrong.

The minute their East Coast–West Coast cover ran, I wrote them a letter that said, "You don't even know what you're doing. You don't know your purpose. Why would you even write that story? You created something that doesn't exist. You're promoting something out of nothing." Then the story got picked up by all the non-rap media. The mainstream media saw a full-time hip-hop magazine reporting on it, so they believed it must be true. Then they followed up on it 'cause it sounded interesting. For a couple of years every interview I gave ended up being about this so-called East Coast–West Coast war: "Mr. Simmons, what do you think of the hip-hop coastal war?" Over and over. And I would always say, "There is no East Coast–West Coast war. What the fuck are you talking about?" Looking back, I think I should have done more to cool things down. I made a couple of calls to Puff and Suge about getting together, but I never really pressed it. At the time I didn't own up to being the oldest person in the whole fucking community. I was 38 at the time. I felt young. But I knew Suge and I knew Puffy, and I should have gotten more in the middle. I regret that. I really do.

What I ultimately did was help get Minister Louis Farrakhan of the Nation of Islam to have a meeting at his home in Chicago. Rappers and industry people from both coasts came to the Minister's home, heard him speak, had something to eat and then chilled with each other. That meeting, along with the shock of Tupac's and Biggie's deaths, cooled everybody off and helped squash the rhetoric. In the end, the controversy and the deaths made this one of the saddest periods in hip-hop's history.

CENSORSHIP AS MARKETING

The rise of West Coast hip-hop brought a lot of calls for the censorship of hip-hop. We'd gone through a period of this in the '80s when Tipper Gore helped organize the Parents Music Resource Center and got the record industry to put warning stickers on albums. The PMRC beef originally started over rock, but it was rap acts like our Slick Rick and L.A.'s Ice-T who felt the brunt of the attacks. It was hip-hop acts who primarily ended up having to record "clean" (aka censored) versions of their work to get placement in many mainstream retail chains, which was both an added expense and an infringement on the act's artistic voice. Then in the '90s we had the conservative Republicans and black people like C. DeLores Tucker attacking record distributors for selling hip-hop, getting press and organizing hearings in Congress. They generated lots of noise and raised the public profile of Tucker, William Bennett and other reactionaries.

But both these movements had the same effect on hip-hop— they were great for the culture and the business.

Attacks like these just reaffirmed to kids that hip-hop was their music. Youth culture and young people always question the norm. These attacks made it clear that rap still stood outside the norm, which made it even more attractive to kids. Personally, I've never been offended by a record. There are some that are more vile than others. But I've always felt the market creates a counterbalance. If you watched the top ten countdown on BET or MTV, even at the height of West Coast rap, you weren't gonna see more than two truly aggressive records.

Moreover, I feel like the rawness of the records had a positive impact. For instance, after years of hearing rappers talk negatively about women, about their babies' mothers and sex, there's been a real change in the patterns of teen pregnancy. Teen pregnancy in the black community is down, and I believe hip-hop—working as the "black CNN," as Chuck D predicted—made girls much smarter about premartial sex. The raps made young girls become less naive and more aware of the attitudes of the guys they're deal- ing with. They may have taken away the innocence of some of the girls who heard them, but there was valuable information for them in those records—information that affected their behavior. Of course, the drop in teen pregnancy was caused by many fac- tors, but these reality-based records actually did what their critics suggested—they affected how young women saw the world, just not in the way those disconnected from the culture thought.

The nastiest record can also be the most educational. If you're a kid and you're really into the culture, there's a lot to be learned from the records. Despite what those outside the culture think, regular hip-hop buyers aren't idiots who turn on the radio, hear a few words and then run out and do what the records say. They understand the context and the artistic intent better than any congressperson or old-school activist.

The trickiest situation we had at Def Jam was over the South Central Cartel. A cop was shot, and the shooter blamed the incident on having listened to the group's album *N Gatz We Truss*. I remember sitting down with the members of the group and asking them what the album's title meant to them. They said, "The reason we only trust our gats is because we don't trust nobody in the streets. All the things that are out there to help and guide us, we don't trust. We trust our gats because we control them." Eventually that case went away. No one kills someone because a record told them to.

I never felt pressure from the anti-rap people to the degree that I was afraid someone was gonna shut me down. The worst-case scenario would be that our distributor would wash its hands of the label and give it back to me. But it never got that heavy. What C. DeLores Tucker did was make rap more visible as the voice of youth. As stupid as she was, Tucker just made all the stars bigger than they were in the eyes of their fans.

I never talked to the censorship suckers. I had no reason to. I didn't have anything to defend. I didn't feel threatened by them. When I saw the negative press, I always felt we'd sell more records because of them. And we did.

In the 2000 presidential election campaign I supported the Gore-Lieberman ticket against George Bush. But both the Democrats and the Republicans used musicians as scapegoats for violence. Whoever is in the White House will have to realize that they can't stop the music. What they should be focusing on is changing the conditions that inspire the music they don't like. If you want better songs, give people better things to write about.

More education, more opportunity and more spirituality will change the music because the culture reflects those changes. Politicians will never stop the truth from coming out. The truth is what these musicians, whether directly or through metaphor, rap about, and that's why they're so popular.

The other thing politicians don't understand or trust is that musicians who don't tell the truth always disappear. Admittedly there are A&R directors who think that negativity sells and therefore promote it. But they are misleading their artists, and in the long run it's usually the artists who suffer.

There is still a void in the market for positive poets. When I arranged a meeting with hip-hop executives and Minister Farrakhan, he had one question for them: "Is Lauryn Hill still popular?" The fact was, she was more popular than all the acts all the executives in the room worked with.

The point is that honesty and integrity sell over a long period of time, and those who blindly follow trends always fall. If your whole foundation is negativity, then you're recording records like a drug dealer, and sooner or later you're gonna get killed or caught.

14 BIGGER AND DEFFER

After ending our once profitable, later acrimonious ten-year relationship with Sony, Def Jam started its relationship with PolyGram in 1994 by bringing them one of the biggest singles and albums in our history. Warren G's "Regulate" sold in the millions, and his debut album, *Regulate . . . G Funk Era,* topped four and a half million copies. Yet from the start our dealings with PolyGram head Alain Levy and the company's top management were rough and rugged.

When we signed with them they had a marketing division called PolyGram Group Marketing that would allow every label under their corporate umbrella to plug into it equally. PGM would prioritize the records as they saw fit, but they had no incentive to work one label's record harder than the other. We loved this idea and saw it as a way to guarantee that our records wouldn't get lost in PolyGram's stew of labels. Unfortunately, the minute we got there they dismantled PGM and put Def Jam under the distribution thumb of another label, Island, which would handle marketing and promotion.

Island had all the incentive in the world to work their records and no incentive at all to work ours. If one of our records came out on June 1 and one of theirs on June 2, which do you think got maximum effort? We lost a lot of hit records because of this arrangement. Matter of fact, we lost much of the product that came out through Warren G's G-Funk label, which we were distributing. Warren had a group, the Twins, who were stars that got lost. He had another group, Dove Shack, that had a sure-thing number one pop record that Island never bothered to work.

So, despite paying $35 million for rights to the most valuable brand in hip-hop, PolyGram didn't respect us. They moved us around from company to company. After we balked at how Island treated us, they put us with Danny Goldberg at Mercury, which was ridiculous, since Mercury had no more reason to promote our product than Island had. No matter the label, the problem was the same: For the heads of the labels there was little profit in working our product—not when they could spend their time on their own.

The problem never got corrected while Alain Levy was running PolyGram. We felt PolyGram was actually killing Def Jam instead of saving it. Lyor and I were so frustrated by the situation that we were actually thinking about selling the company. We began thinking we should sell Def Jam, take some of its assets and then go to another distributor and start fresh with a company totally committed to us.

In February 1998 we had pretty much negotiated a deal to sell Def Jam to PolyGram for $50 million. Then PolyGram tried to get us to accept $34 million because we had taken some advances. For instance, PolyGram had agreed to invest in Phat Farm, but later made it a loan. They also tried to charge us back for a movie I used an advance against my back-end royalties to finance, *The Addiction*. They tried to charge us back for all kinds of shit. So they cut $16 million off the $50 million offer for Def Jam to pay back the charges. My lawyer was calling my house, telling me I would be stupid not to take the deal.

At the same time Lyor and I had offers to go a lot of places and run a company. If we'd sold Def Jam for $50 million, we could have gotten $25 million or more to go somewhere else and start over. But then we had a fight with PolyGram over wanting to take DMX and Jay-Z with us. If Lyor and I were leaving, we wanted to do so with some of what we were building. So that delayed the deal.

But the real stumbling block was our separation anxiety. Throughout the whole negotiation our lawyers were yelling, "You should take this $34 million or this $50 million." But we kept saying, "Fuck you!" I mean, that's nice money, but it's definitely not the $130 million we eventually sold 40 percent of Def Jam for in 1998. Our reluctance to leave behind acts like DMX and Jay-Z delayed the deal and ultimately worked to our benefit.

The $100 million difference was made by how quickly we were growing. Between the first offer and what we finally got, two things happened—our distribution problems were worked out and we did some great A&R. After Seagram bought PolyGram in 1998 and merged it with MCA, we got more direct control of our distribution. No more middlemen. No more second-class treatment. A lot more hits.

The second thing is that we got better at recognizing and nurturing talent. Though Def Jam in the '80s was a very special, groundbreaking label, it actually made more money and had bigger hits in the '90s. We had a downturn at the beginning of the '90s, but since then we've broken Method Man, Redman, Foxy Brown, Montell Jordan, Jay-Z and DMX while continuing with EPMD, returning Slick Rick to the market, and acquiring Sisqo, Dru Hill and Kelly Price.

In fact, we've had a second golden era at Def Jam. Now we are no longer the coolest, hottest new kid on the block. We are an institution, and in a business as trend-conscious as youth culture, that can be a dangerous place. People root for the underdog, and we are no longer that. Because we've expanded the market, there is more competition for acts, for promotions on radio and for video spots on MTV. But in spite of greater competition than ever, Def Jam is still on top.

LYOR'S TEAM

We've survived and thrived into the twenty-first century because of the staff and the corporate culture at Def Jam, elements nurtured primarily by Lyor Cohen. I go back to the signing of Warren G as a defining moment, both for the company and for Lyor. Warren was a guest MC on and the producer of Mr. Grimm's "Indo Smoke," the single off the *Boyz N the Hood* sound track. Lyor saw the video and was asking everybody, "Who's that guy? No, not Mr. Grimm. The guy next to him." He was told it was

Warren G. Lyor got on a plane, chased him down and signed him. After that Lyor and Def Jam never looked back.

Up until that point Lyor had never gotten a chance to exercise his love of hip-hop. As a manager, he'd had great relations with the acts he had and had some input into picking singles. But once he got comfortable at Def Jam he blossomed as a record man. He became great at signing acts, developing them and following through with great marketing.

He'd learned the business exactly as I had—going on the road with acts and working outside the building. Lyor worked really hard and never tried to promote himself. His equity in Def Jam developed because I'd give him a bigger share before it got unfair. I've always tried to protect my business relationships by not exploiting people. The idea is to have relationships where you make money and the other guy makes money, too. That's how a business keeps its team together. When you run a business with that goal in mind, the people who work for you don't ask you for anything, because they know they'll end up with a fair deal if they just work hard.

As Lyor was growing at Def Jam, I was busy with Phat Farm, *Def Comedy Jam*, Rush Media and my movie ventures. I was distracted with other projects, and it allowed Lyor a wider lane to move in. The truth is, the more I got away from Def Jam on a day-to-day basis, the better the company did. So Lyor was the most critical part of the success.

Just as Lyor had developed acts at Rush, he has excelled at developing executive talent at Def Jam. The current president of Def Jam, Kevin Liles, started at the company as an intern. Lyor started to work with him and gave him direction, and the next thing I knew, we were talking about making Kevin president of the company. He worked his way up pretty quickly, from intern to member of the street team to a regional promotion position to head of national promotion.

When we offered him the job as president, Kevin didn't know if he wanted it. He was worried about the corporate culture at Def Jam and whether some of our other young executives, like head of marketing Julie Greenwald or head of business affairs Todd Moscowitz, who were also young and aggressive, would be uncomfortable reporting to him, since he was a peer.

But it's worked out fine, because Kevin is not about grandstanding or showing off. He doesn't look for credit. He doesn't wanna have his photo taken. He just wants to be effective. It's a unique quality today in a kid who came up from the street and who had to hustle his way up. That attitude of Kevin's is exactly why his appointment worked.

Throughout our history Def Jam has been an industry leader in marketing hip-hop, and in the '90s our staff came up with some truly innovative campaigns. A good example is what Julie Greenwald, whom I consider a marketing genius, came up with when Redman and Method Man began collaborating. It was her concept to link the release of two of their albums as the "Month of the Man." That campaign built consumer awareness for both albums, linked the two MCs and popularized a collaboration that has resulted in several hit records.

Another very effective Def Jam marketing campaign was the Survival of the Illest tour. Much like in the days of the Rush

Productions tours, we put together a promotion that included Onyx, DMX and some other real aggressive acts. In a period when jiggy, smoothed-out images were hot, the promotion and a subsequent tour reaffirmed Def Jam's tradition of edgy, raw hip-hop. It also was a key element in establishing DMX as a star, since he was featured in the promotion and headlined the tour. We even did a live album called *Survival of the Illest*. It wasn't a big seller, but it solidified in the audience's mind that DMX was not just another MC, but an artist who could rock any stage.

One of the company's strengths comes from the fact that for most of our staff, Def Jam is the first and only job they've had. For Kevin, Julie and Todd Def Jam is their first real job out of college. Lyor has never worked anywhere else. Wes "Party" Johnson, who is our senior vice president of promotion, was an independent before affiliating with us. Most of the people in our office only have Def Jam on their resume. The tradition in the record business is that people are gypsies. They move from company to company, trying to get bigger salaries. But we keep people by paying them fairly and providing an environment that's supportive. That's how you develop a good corporate culture. That's why when I walk through Def Jam's offices it still feels like an independent company, because we've maintained an entrepreneurial, aggressive mentality.

BLOWIN' UP THE SPOT

Heat comes and goes. A record label might have a staff that's aggressive and competitive and wants to be better than everyone else out there. Or they might have a staff that gets lost. That's the funny thing about the creative process in companies like Def Jam. People just get on a streak, start competing among themselves and then aspire to higher levels. The reason we signed great acts is because we did a better job of identifying commercial talent than everyone else. When it came to hip-hop, the majors didn't know what they were doing, so it didn't matter how much money they had.

We got Method Man as a solo act out of the Wu-Tang Clan because Tracy Waples, an A&R director I hired, brought him to me when there was nothing out from Wu-Tang but an Ol' Dirty Bastard record on the A side of a 12-inch and on the B side "Method Man," a song no one had even heard yet. Tracy did her job—identifying star-quality talent—and we did ours, signing him and developing him as a solo recording artist.

Irv Gotti, who found DMX for us, is a guy from my old hood, Hollis, Queens, who had been in the street. Word of mouth on Irv was strong—it said he knew some shit. First he brought us Ja Rule, who would later record a million-selling album for us. Lyor brought him in. We listened to the records he played for us and saw his enthusiasm for the music and the culture. We felt his vibe. So we hired him, and immediately he brought us DMX, who's had three number one pop albums in a row.

It's got so that when we pick an act we're ready to sign, every other label wants to chase it. While we were in the middle of negotiating with Roc-A-Fella records for Jay-Z and their roster, Sony showed up and tried to throw their wallet in the way. It's like they follow our A&R people around and if we like it, then they pursue it. It happens all the time. But, as in the case of Roc-A-Fella, we usually get acts we really want because of our understanding of the market and our track record of success.

I think successful A&R people are cultural observers as much as they are music people. They know what's going on. They know when something feels right from an attitude standpoint. Sometimes in judging MCs it's not about the poetry, but about the vocal inflections and physical attitude. Sometimes I can look at rappers and tell just by their hand movements and the look in their eyes, whether they're special or not—just like seeing how a guy holds a basketball tells you whether he's a real player or not.

As a result of all our activity, in 1997 we grossed about $60 million. We looked at 1998 and figured we'd gross $80 million Then we looked at our numbers again and said, "We're gonna do $100 million this year!" We ended up doing $185 million in 1998. In 1999 we did $250 million. So the whole time we were arguing with PolyGram over the sale of Def Jam, our billing increased, our value increased and the sale price more than doubled.

By all standards we made a killing selling Def Jam to PolyGram in 1999, yet from an entrepreneurial standpoint, it's not a good thing that we now have employment contracts instead of owning the company outright. Lyor is now president of Island/Def Jam, an entity composed of several labels, including Def Jam. I'm chairman of Def Jam, and Kevin Liles is now its president. At the time of the sale we all could actually have gone out and started a new company or go run another company and made even more money. Lyor and myself are worth a lot as executives.

But in all honesty, I feel much better that we stayed with our artists at Def Jam. That was the problem with selling the company in the first place. How was I gonna be without Redman, Method Man and Slick Rick? I like the artists. I talk to them a lot about their lives and careers. I'm the CEO or the chairman or whatever. Like the old man says in *Citizen Kane,* "It's something to do." And without Def Jam, Lyor would go crazy.

I love Ja Rule. I love DMX. I love Jay-Z. I love L.L. Cool J, Erick Sermon, Redman, Method Man. These are my peeps. I love the singer Case—I signed him—how can I leave him behind? I helped sign Montel Jordan. Foxy Brown I love like my daughter. I love Damon Dash, the CEO of Roc-A-Fella. Plus my other ventures help market them, be it putting someone in a Phat Farm TV ad or putting artists' images on the side of a Mystic soft drink bottle through dRush. Every day I work for Def Jam. I do it as part of my life process. That's why I'm better off staying.

JAY-Z
AND DMX

In the '90s hip-hop has gone from an underground experience where people discovered the music to an experience that's marketed to them, yet I believe the best experience is still the underground one. It's the music that people discover for themselves that means the most to them. That's how DMX developed. The same with Jay-Z. We've been lucky at Def Jam to have them come out of the underground as they have.

Jay-Z, for example, was on a small independent label out of

Brooklyn, Roc-A-Fella, and he grew into stardom with Def Jam's help. He's not a visual artist, like Busta Rhymes. His rhymes mean everything. MTV didn't make Jay-Z; Jay-Z's skills made him. DMX is similar in that respect. He'd been around the New York hip-hop scene for a while, working with a crew of MCs from Yonkers that included the Lox. For DMX, as dynamic-looking as he is, videos mean nothing. His persona and skills are what made him.

DMX is a great poet, a great artist and a raw talent. He deserves the stardom. I've heard people try to label him a Tupac imitator. Well, the only thing they have in common is that they can wake up on two sides of the same bed and that they are profound poets. Both of their work will be taught in colleges fifty years from now because they write about the culture, not just the flavor of the minute.

Jay-Z writes about very specific cultural things—the right coat, the right shoes, the right car to have right at this moment. What are we aspiring to have in the ghetto? What language is slickest right now? Jay-Z, like the late Biggie Smalls, defines our times. He has something to say about what's happening all around him, and does it with great wordplay. That kind of skill is a subtle thing. It's amazing that Jay can describe everyday things in cool, original ways that make you look at them in a completely new way.

In contrast, DMX talks about finding meaning in suffering. In his rhymes he suggests that God may not be there when you want him, but he's always on time. DMX talks to the devil on record. He talks to God on record. One hundred years ago storytelling about the battle between the devil and God, good and evil, held people's attention, and it still does. DMX deals with the spiritual struggle in a material world.

On my yoga altar I put up photographs of different people. Minister Farrakhan is up there because he means well and is close to God. Glinda the Good Witch is up there because she represents absolute good, right? We know nothing bad about Glinda the Good Witch. And I have DMX up there. He cries all the time because he knows he's done wrong. In yoga you practice being good, but with the knowledge that you fuck up every day. You practice being better. DMX is practicing really hard at being good—he's just really fucked up. But he keeps trying.

His records, *It's Dark and Hell Is Hot* and *Flesh of My Flesh, Blood of My Blood,* are about being in pain. He's sorry for any evil he's done. He's frustrated at his inability to change. Every time he gets a glimpse of something good, he wants to change and become good. But he just can't stay on the right path. "I've done bad but I'm gonna be good"—that's his message. If all you heard was DMX from age one through adulthood, you'd end up a saint, because his music is about navigating that line between good and evil.

If from age one to adulthood all you heard was Jay-Z, you're gonna learn to get ahead of everybody and fight the world. You're gonna learn to kill. You know what? A baby will go right to hell fuckin' with Jay-Z, but that baby will be wearing the hottest designer shit and driving the hottest car with the coolest rims.

And that's why they matter so much. DMX will take you to heaven, and Jay-Z will take you right to hell.

BLACK POP VERSUS WHITE RESISTANCE

The selling of hip-hop music changed so much in the last part of the '90s. Some of the things that we went through at Def Jam don't have to happen to the younger black entrepreneurs coming up now. But at the same time we're still dealing with the ignorance and arrogance of white executives who don't want us to win—not because we aren't making their companies money, but because they're just uncomfortable with the culture. At the level hip-hop's at now, we no longer deal with the young, alternative white guys who ran indie labels and embraced the culture for its rebel nature. Now we're dealing with older white men, products of mainstream pop, who will never be totally comfortable with hip-hop.

I remember when we brought Onyx's "Slam" over to MTV and were told, "The act is too threatening and too scary." I said, "No. This is a pop record. Why is this any more threatening than a record by an alternative band?" I thought "Slam" was the most perfect MTV video ever made. It had attitude, energy and aggression, with Onyx, all bald-headed black guys, nearly bouncing off the walls as they rhymed. It was very young, very rock and roll. It was probably the first hip-hop mosh pit video. But the MTV programmers were all scared of the band. Eventually it did get on MTV and became a number one request. A lot of people in this industry don't realize that kids are more open-minded than they believe. When these executives say shit like, "The audience won't understand it," what they really mean is that they don't get it. They're trying to think for the audience, but they get it wrong. They act as if the whole world, especially kids, are more racist than they are.

A lot of white executives enjoy promoting music they understand, music that makes them culturally comfortable. They like to be able to make a decision on something that they feel in their heart. So despite the fact that there's a generation of rock-and-roll people who love rap 'cause they grew up with it, too, the men who control the major record companies and pop radio have never been comfortable with hip-hop. They're 50-year-old white men who are so happy working Britney Spears, the Backstreet Boys and all that teen pop right now. That they understand.

Andre Harrell's career as a label head at Uptown and Motown illustrates how white executives have underestimated and hampered the growth of hip-hop. As I said earlier, Andre started as a rapper, then he worked for me at Rush Management. In 1986 he left me to start a joint venture with MCA records called Uptown. At MCA Andre had a horrible deal structure, similar to what I had at Sony. The deal simply wasn't profitable for him, though it was great for MCA. Uptown was the most important label in their whole building. Once he'd developed hit acts like Heavy D, Guy, Mary J. Blige and Jodeci (from which K-Ci & JoJo emerged), they couldn't wait to take over his operation.

To them Andre was trouble because he knew he had a bunch of acts that should have gone pop. Uptown released "Stay" and "Forever My Lady" by Jodeci, and many great early Mary J. Blige records that MCA never really promoted aggressively as pop records. Between Guy and Heavy D and Soul for Real, along with Jodeci and Mary J., Uptown should have had as many huge pop singles as Def Jam, but there was no commitment there from the parent company. MCA kept Uptown in a box called "urban" when it should have been much more. In their minds, since MCA only owned half of Uptown, they didn't have any reason to help him build his company. They just figured Uptown was a good little moneymaker that filled a niche.

So Andre used to hate the top executives at MCA, and he had every right to. They made him drop Biggie Smalls because MCA hated what they thought Biggie represented. They pressured Andre every day to push Puffy out. So Andre would scream at them. He let them know how whack the talent on MCA was overall and how much Uptown meant to their bottom line. So MCA pushed him out of Uptown in 1996 and smeared him as a bad, irresponsible executive. Yet here we are in the twenty first century and MCA, which took over Andre's Uptown acts, is still living off Mary J. and K-Ci & JoJo. When it comes to black creative executives, these companies just use them up and throw them away. To them black executives are disposable.

So I helped Andre get the job of running Motown records for PolyGram in 1996. In getting that job, Andre finally got paid the money he should have made at Uptown. Financially the job was fine. He made $30 million in eighteen months. But spiritually it was terrible for him. They fired him after a year and a half. They blamed him for all of PolyGram's ills when the real problem was always Alain Levy and his management of the talent he acquired. Levy couldn't get along with Chris Blackwell at Island. He couldn't get along with me. He couldn't get along with Herb Alpert and Jerry Moss at A&M. And he couldn't get along with Andre Harrell. See the pattern? He didn't respect true entrepreneurs.

From the day you sign an act to the day you put it out takes an average of about two years. Andre had eighteen months, and PolyGram was forcing him to release a lot of records before they were set up properly. They were leaking negative stuff to the media about him. During that period I was living in Andre's apartment when I was in New York, and I saw him working from eight in the morning till ten at night. He'd have marketing meetings at two in the morning sometimes. He worked harder during that period than he ever had at Uptown.

Yet overall PolyGram was so cold, they used him as one of the scapegoats for a label that had lost $70 million the year before he got there. He lost $80 million for his one fiscal year after dropping most of the roster, firing and hiring a whole new staff and relocating the company. The restructuring itself cost $20 million. Andre needed at least another year to allow his records to come out and be properly positioned, but they didn't give him enough time.

Andre's major fault at Motown was that he talked too much and overpromoted himself. Rappers always brag about their skills, their clothes, their car, etc. Andre was a rapper-as-executive talking about the record company he was gonna make. He was being true to his background and the culture by letting the world know: "Motown has got new, young people running it from the hip-hop generation." It was not a bad strategy. But by making himself the star he pissed people off, especially a subtle Frenchman like Levy. Once they saw that Andre had made the cover of *New York* magazine they grew jealous.

I'll never forget a presentation he did for the PolyGram group. Andre played a video in which he pulled up in his green Bentley in front of the Motown Cafe, walked in and started interviewing his new acts. He turned to the camera and said to a roomful of European executives, "Yeah, I'm getting ready to take Motown and be outta here." These guys were either shocked or appalled at Andre's boasting because culturally they just weren't used to it. Andre came in there with a vision, an attitude. He was confident and hungry. Then he had a couple of records that didn't hit and they started bricking with him so much, it must have taken the confidence out of him. Levy couldn't take Andre. The green Bentley was just too much for him.

After the Motown thing, none of the big companies would hire Andre. The scumbags in this business, who recycle white executives like returnable bottles, wouldn't give him a shot. He ended up running Bad Boy for Puffy for three years. I'm not bitter about most things, but Andre's situation upsets me.

P.S.: In 2001 Andre and Kenneth "Babyface" Edmonds have started a new label together—game recognizes game.

PURE PLAYAS

The good side of what's happened with this culture is that the younger generation is getting paid now without having to wait. Young black people are entrepreneurs now. White A&R directors sign five hundred acts that sell millions of records, but they still just get paychecks. Irv Gotti, the man who brought us DMX, got $3 million and his own label. The reason? The people in these buildings can't do what Irv Gotti can do. They didn't pay us before, but now black creative executives have to be paid because white executives have no idea how to do what they do. I know in the minds of the white executives it's getting out of hand.

The Cash Money clique, the people behind the Hot Boys and Juvenile, who have exploded out of New Orleans, don't have to worry about a relationship like the ones Def Jam and Uptown had with the big record companies, 'cause they own their whole operation. They're getting ready to get richer than me and Lyor got, and they're kids. They are young black ghetto businessmen with a make-it-for-a-penny-sell-it-for-a-dollar thought process. They're smart enough to know they don't need Universal to make money. They know they don't need partners.

When you have a hot company—a No Limit or Cash Money—all the majors can do is suck your dick. As I said earlier in the book in reference to my career, a hot record opens all the doors. If Universal doesn't like the deal, Sony likes it. If Sony doesn't like it, BMG does. These guys can't speak the king's English, but they can buy and sell most every white record executive in America. Master P, a man with a mouth full of gold, is one of the richest people in the country under 40. He owns his shit. The guys who run Cash Money own their label. Tony Draper, who runs Suave House out of Houston, owns his company. What happens now is that the majors have to pay them for the right to distribute their records.

These aren't joint ventures. These are deals to distribute music made by two companies that come in as equals. These labels had already sold records themselves on the underground tip, and they have been smart about maintaining their equity control. I love the image of these Harvard guys sitting across from these southern boys with gold fronts in their mouths, having to give in because they want and need to be in business with them. It's the best punk rock explosion of all time. In fact, it's ten times greater than anything punk rock ever achieved.

RAISING PUFFY

Look at the rise of Puffy. When Andre introduced me to Sean Combs in 1988, he was just a young, skinny kid who thought he knew everything. But he also listened a lot. So he was there as an intern at Uptown, poised to learn, aggressive and hardworking. He was up under Andre all the time. I'd be talking and look up and it was like the kid was in my mouth. That motherfucker would be paying attention!

Then he just started doing incredible stuff. Andre would give him some direction, and Puffy would go all the way with it. He fine-tuned the attitude at Uptown, making it younger and edgier. For example, Puffy steered the vocal group Jodeci away from looking like the band Guy— another Uptown act—which had a kind of smoothed-out R&B look. Puffy made Jodeci look totally hip-hop with baggy clothes and Timberland boots. Puffy worked with them as if he was a member of the group and developed their imagery, so that Jodeci blended soul group vocals with hip-hop style. Puffy gave them an image that was commercial and cutting edge for a vocal group. But it was Andre who matched them with

Al B. Sure!, Uptown's first star, who produced that first album, which established the group. At Uptown the team of a senior person and a young creative person worked. When Puffy left Uptown in 1994 and formed Bad Boy, everything that he learned at Uptown was taken to another level. Partly that's because Arista made Bad Boy a corporate priority. And partly that's because Puffy is one of the most talented people in the game. But Puffy was groomed and trained in the business, and it was Andre Harrell who did that for him. The best story I have that tells you who Puffy is goes back to when he first came to New York. At that time I was on the StairMaster every day. I was addicted to it. So Puffy got on the StairMaster for the first time in his life and made me a bet. If he could stay on it longer than I could, I'd fix his Volkswagen. If he couldn't, he'd give me $500. He was sweating bullets after three minutes, but he would not get off the machine. I wanted to win, too, but I wasn't gonna stay on it to the point where I couldn't walk the next day. Puffy, however, was prepared to go the distance—and he did. The motherfucker was sweating and screaming, "What! What!" That's Puffy, highly competitive and willing to outwork anybody. That's why he wins.

Puffy's still yelling. He's still aggressive and hardworking. Despite all the negativity out there about him, he's not gonna be Hammer—a phenomenon that rises quickly and then disappears. No matter what the media want or the industry wants or the Manhattan district attorney wants, Puffy's not going away. He's gonna be successful for a long time as a businessperson. Bad Boy has made the transition that Def Jam made, from being associated with one specific sound or trend to being a successful, consistent institution that spans many trends. That's a transition few companies have made.

RAP, LIVE AND VIDEOTAPE

Another way that the hip-hop game has changed in recent years is that the concert business is not nearly as important to an artist's career as it used to be. Until the '80s concerts were the most significant way to touch the audience and break new acts. Not anymore.

In hip-hop the change began in the late '80s, when the whole gold-chain era turned into the snatching-gold-chain era. The atmosphere at many shows became a bit dangerous. The truth is that hip-hop parties were always a little bit dangerous. Back in the '70s niggers would get shot in Disco Fever and be lying on the floor. The body would be dragged off the floor, and an hour later you partied again.

Ultimately the violence wasn't really about or caused by hip-hop. It was about teenage energy and the lack of respect for life that the ghetto breeds. I remember when I was 16 years old I'd go to the RKO Alden in Queens to see shows, and every so often the Seven Crowns and my gang, the Seven Immortals, would come and rip up the whole theater. The shows back then usually featured R&B ballad groups like the Detroit Emeralds or the Delphonics. There used to be this MC, Sad Sam, who hosted all the shows wearing hot pants. Sad Sam would come onstage and yell, "Y'all niggers sit down! Stop fighting, motherfuckers!" This was years before the big hip-hop concerts. Of course, the difference between two thousand in the RKO Alden and twenty thousand in Madison Square Garden is pretty dramatic. The policing of the larger spaces became difficult. But that's the problem with any large gathering of teenagers. People always use the term "rap violence" whenever there's an incident at a rap show. But I'm sure they had "blues violence" and "jazz violence," and we know they had "rock violence."

People like to blame the music for kids' problems when it's the kids with problems who create the music and, unfortunately, create the violence as well. Whether a gangster or just a kid with a thug mentality beat someone at a concert or out in the street, it has nothing to do with the music. The violence was a result of the larger environment. Rap is part of that culture—it didn't create it. When concert violence in the late '80s became an issue, Run-D.M.C. was rapping about how kids should "go to school or the church." Even back then, with black hats and leather pants on, they were talking about being good and God-fearing. All they ever rhymed about was positive shit.

Yet one of the most notorious incidents in hip-hop history happened at a Run-D.M.C. show in Long Beach, California, in 1983. Run wasn't even onstage when several gangs decided to have a rumble right inside the arena. It was a gang beef that happened to erupt at our concert. Gang shootings were happening all over L.A. at that time, but because this particular incident happened at a concert venue, it went from being "gang violence" to being "rap violence," like the gangsters heard a Run-D.M.C. song and decided to attack a kid wearing another color. How ridiculous is that?

The perception of "rap violence" affected the concert business because it made parents keep their kids from coming out. It made kids afraid to come out. The insurance companies and the buildings raised their fees so high, it became impossible to take tours on the road.

It wasn't just violence that changed touring. When Run-D.M.C. and Whodini were selling out arenas, all the cool kids in town had to be there. Now concerts are a less significant part of nightlife. You don't have to go to shows anymore to be cool. Rock bands don't even tour the way they used to in the '80s. The Hard Knock Life tour that Jay-Z and DMX headlined so successfully in 1999 sold out over forty dates, but they were selling tickets to a less streetwise, younger, more racially mixed, more middle-class group than the tours of the '80s attracted. The energy at the shows is different because the audiences are.

The truth is, hip-hop now sells more records with fewer live appearances. The difference is that back then, the average fan had few ways to see our artists. In the '80s you didn't even know what they looked like. You wanna meet Kurtis Blow? You wanna watch his mannerisms? You wanna see what kind of gear he might be wearing? If you wanted to see the actual artists and understand the culture better, you had to wait for the concert to come through.

Now videos have replaced concerts. Every couple of hours on television you see performances by your favorite artists for free. The videos today are often multimillion-dollar productions, carefully designed to present the look that the artist wants to sell. They present the most flattering image the artist, the director, the stylist and the record company can create. Back in the day the most dramatic image available was Kurtis Blow's picture on a 12-inch sleeve.

Busy Bee is a legendary hip-hop MC and DJ. Back when he was hot, in the early '80s, you might have been buying rap records your whole life and still you wouldn't know what Busy Bee looked like. You could only dream about what Busy Bee or Melle Mel looked like unless you saw a concert. Now you watch them on your favorite video channel. So why go to the concert?

I came into the business just as the transition from concerts to videos was happening, so I have some mixed feelings about the change. The whole time a music video is running, it's supposed to be giving viewers a feeling for the performer. The video is telling you why you, the viewer, should like the artist. It's supposed to be winning people over.

Selling an artist is like running for president. The voter/fan is looking at every move the candidate/artist makes so he can determine whether he likes the candidate/artist or not. Issues come and go, but a good president doesn't adapt his whole image to fit one issue. Same in selling an artist. Artists should not compromise their whole image to fit one song.

If you make videos so viewers will like one song, you're wasting time and money. Videos are expensive, so every time viewers see an act's video it should make them excited about the artist, not just the song. You can make a hit video, yet harm the artist's image through that video. You really have to be careful about the imagery involved.

If you're Busta Rhymes and you're known for making highly theatrical videos, then it's okay to make extravagant pieces because the audience knows that's what Busta Rhymes does. But sometimes you see artists and their images different every time because they're trying to make their look match the song. I think that's wrong. I think people who buy records don't give a fuck about that.

The Wu-Tang videos that cost seven grand, like "Bring the Pain" and "Method Man," were the best for that crew. The least effective video they ever did was one my friend Brett Ratner made that cost a million and had tons of special effects. It was too much to watch. It wasn't about Wu-Tang—it was about special effects. They're not that band. They had guts. They had a following. Instead of making you vote for them, the more expensive video had you asking for a recount.

15 SPIRITUAL MATTERS

My younger brother, Joey, is now the ordained minister Reverend Run—the latest evolution in a long, complicated life. His most popular sermon is about a particular day at the peak of his success when he sat in a Jacuzzi getting his hair cut, eating pancakes, smoking a joint, and waiting for a ho to call. He says, "The syrup was falling into the tub, ashes were falling into the pancakes, and I'm waitin' on a ho to call. I thought I had all the riches, but I was really poor. It was then the Lord came into my life and raised me up, and I started to feel better and all those worldly things didn't mean anything to me anymore."

Similarly, the practice of yoga has changed my life. Over the past six years I've been practicing yoga, and in that time found a spiritual center to my life. My spiritual sense is stronger than ever, so the teachings of all the great religions sound good to me. The yoga practice of quieting the mind through asana practice, as well as meditation, is about clearing the mind of fluctuation so that you can one day know your true self. The Buddhists refer to this state as *nirvana*, the Yogis as *samadhi* or, simply, *state of yoga*. The key, regardless of the religious path you follow, is to look inward for happiness. My experiences with yoga have taught me the practice of finding God everywhere—especially within myself.

My good friend Bobby Shriver got me into yoga in the mid-90s when I was living in Los Angeles. He took me to a class taught by former monk Steve Ross out in Brentwood, which was full of beautiful actresses, supermodels, and an heir or two. That was the main reason I went. Looking back, Steve was also the perfect introduction to yoga for a person like me. He's a deeply spiritual person, but he also takes things very lightly. He plays Tupac and R&B records in class. He'll come over and whisper about how many fine girls are in class while you're in Downward Dog (an asana position), whereas most teachers might tell you not to look at the girls. Funny, I started out chasing pussy at Amaha Yoga in L.A. and somehow that has led to a practice I do every day at Jivamukti in New York. The definitive textbook or "bible" of yoga is *The Yoga Sutras of Patanjali* by Sri Swami Satchidananda, a book that I have read cover to cover numerous times. The exact date when it was written is unknown, but is estimated to be 5,000 years ago. Its teachings have become my greatest inspiration.

One of the practices of yoga is to cause the least amount of harm possible to all sentient beings and the planet. That has led me to become a vegan. Some yogis say that you can never achieve a state of yoga or *samadhi* (enlightenment) until you become vegan. I believe this and have chosen to eliminate all animal products from my diet. I also believe that, both spiritually and psychically, it is bad for you and the planet to consume any animal products and have found this transition to be natural and easy. If you want to know the numerous ways that eating animals causes harm you should read *Diet for a New America* by John Robbins.

I have learned something else: Life is about finding happiness. It is that simple. As I said, the only real happiness is the kind that comes from within, and I believe that my happiness only comes from serving other people. When I started this book three years ago I was uncomfortable about writing a memoir while I was still so young. Now, I realize the timing is perfect, because while my first forty years were about consumption and money and power, I am hopeful that the years to come will be about service.

This doesn't mean I won't work as hard to promote and achieve my business goals. It only means that in the future I want to contribute more than I take. When I pass, I want my tombstone to read HERE LIES RUSSELL WENDELL SIMMONS—PHILANTHROPIST, not GREEDY ENTREPRENEUR. Over the last few years I have begun to walk toward God or service to God, whether it is through promoting political initiatives that I believe could help the masses— from reforming the prison industrial complex to increased involvement in electoral politics—or by focusing more on the numerous charities I am involved with. I am in a unique position to organize some hip-hop for the better of the masses and have lent my support to such people as Hillary Clinton, Al Gore, Reverend Al Sharpton, Andy Cuomo, Mark Green, and the Honorable Minister Louis Farrakhan. I want to spark young people to be more conscious of, and active in, social and political issues, and I think hip-hop can be a powerful tool for helping young people see the important issues that unite them, instead of the superficial differences that divide them. I have seen my own usefulness and will continue along the path contributing whatever I can to make this a better place.

16 BUSINESS AND LIFE LESSONS

This book has been about where I've been, but it doesn't touch the surface of where I'm going. At this book's publication I'm only 44, and my life has changed so much in just the last few years because of my spiritual practice. My wife, Kimora Lee, and my beautiful baby girl, Ming Lee, have also changed me in very profound ways. And I'm starting so many new businesses with the potential to be bigger than all the things I've done in the past combined.

So in thinking about how to end this book, I figured I'd do it by summing up the business and life lessons I've learned so far. Twenty years from now, when I do my follow-up book, I expect to have learned a lot more, God willing. But these five lessons are what I can pass on now—I hope they are as useful to you as they have been to me.

1. In any new business, someone has to have a vision. You may have the investors. You may know the market exists. But you need a point of view on the business, a definite vision, to pull it all together. The foundation of Def Jam was that hip-hop was teenage music with the same rebel appeal as rock and roll. The foundation of Phat Farm was classic American style and seeing that style in a broader way than other companies had before. Having a vision that drives your business and shapes your decisions is crucial.

2. You are only as good as the people around you. You can have a powerful vision, but without a staff that can make it happen, it's just a dream. I believe the most difficult thing in business is to find smart people and keep them. Lyor Cohen has been with me since the early '80s as a friend and partner. He's shared in all our growth, our setbacks and our successes. I've made sure that Lyor has always been rewarded for his passion and his work. You can't create an enduring enterprise if you don't pay your senior staff what they deserve—you'll lose them like a set of keys.

3. People aren't good or bad—just smart or stupid. In other words, you must try to keep yourself open to people. Don't be too judgmental. Don't make snap judgments. Today's asshole may be tomorrow's innovator. Many of the people I've mentioned in the previous pages were difficult to get along with. Some had a lot of internal anger. Some held unnecessary grudges. Some had nasty personal habits. Ultimately, however, what mattered was their insight and ability to perform their duties. Some companies believe that to be successful, everyone has to have a congenial personality and fit a mold. If that was the case, I never would have made it out of Hollis.

4. Don't try to be all things to all people. Identify your core community and go from there. Sometimes you have to offend a lot of people to excite a lot of people. The people who are excited about what you're doing and who will defend you against those who are offended—those are your core people. From Run-D.M.C. to Public Enemy, from the Beastie Boys to Onyx, from *Def Comedy Jam* to DMX, I've been involved with so many projects that have been vilified, demonized and dissed. And that's been good. The haters have always solidified the fan base for all these projects. Playa haters are some of the best publicists around. Please, keep up the good work.

5. Nothing happens the way it's supposed to. In my experience, it often takes as long as five years to make a business work. Partners can fail you. Staff may not execute properly. You could be too far ahead of the market. So you have to be willing to hang in there and make it happen. From the founding of Phat Farm in 1992 until 1997, I lost money. By my account, I experienced $10 million in losses. But today Phat Farm is visible, it is imitated and it generates hundreds of millions of dollars. It took time, but good ideas often do need time to take off. Being an entrepreneur requires instinct, fortitude and the ability to accept that the world does not run on your schedule. Sometimes you just have to believe.

And as I used to say at the end of *Def Comedy Jam,* "Good night. God bless."

EPILOGUE

ife and Def is the story of how I've gotten to the place I'm at now, but it isn't the story of my life. I plan to dedicate the rest of my life to doing what I can—through my businesses and other initiatives—to help empower people. My recent forays into politics have the same ultimate goal as my ongoing social and philanthropic initiatives, and that's to uplift poor people. A society is measured by the way it treats its poor and, if that's the measure of our humanity and sophistication, then we in the United States are barely human and in no way sophisticated. We treat people— especially poor and working-class people—like shit. As a society, we exploit them, don't educate them, don't provide them with decent health care, and don't promote opportunity to them. We throw them in prisons and try to forget them. I spend a lot of my time and resources these days in supporting movements and activists who will fight this war on ignorance and poverty.

The Hip Hop Summits we've held over the last couple of years are in that spirit. Every significant political movement in the world has been energized by the spirit of young people, and right now a lot of them have become apathetic, through no fault of their own. However, we can't move forward as a country without them. It's the young people who need to tell us how to fix the mess that old people have made. What young people need is a platform for their ideas and an outlet to get involved with in the process of political and social change. *Def Poetry Jam*—the poetry and spoken word series we've launched with HBO—is part of this engagement process. The poets you see on that program, gifted young people like Black Ice, are not marginal, alternative voices; they are instead part of a new wave of artists who are bringing to the American mainstream the language and ideas of the kids in the street. These young poets come out of the same spirit as hip-hop, but without music they're challenged to say something even more profound, something that stands on its own without a hot beat to back it up. The show has been a success so far, and the power of these poets and their poems—their political and social content, their creativity and humor—is the reason the ratings for each show have increased. We're seeing repeats with higher ratings than the original broadcasts, so interest in the show is spreading by word of mouth, which reflects the hunger that's out there for new ideas.

Between the Hip Hop Summits and *Def Poetry Jam*, we're hoping to plant a big seed that will grow into a movement, getting young people to bring their ideas to a positive critical analysis of our society. Putting these ideas out, I believe, will lead hip-hop to aspire to be even greater than it already is. I have no problem with hip-hop today or with the records you hear on the radio right now; I just believe it can be a stronger, more varied medium for our community, and that goal is the driving force for everything we're doing. It is my hope that these activities will one day be viewed as being as meaningful as anything I've done in business. Social activism fills up much of my time, along with my wife, Kimora, and my child, which is why I'm as happy as I've ever been.

Namaste.

INDEX